GOLDEN NUGGETS
Divine Revelations

ISBN: 0692932631
ISBN-13: 978-0692932636 (Soaring Eagle Ministries, Inc.)

Soaring Eagle Ministries, Inc.
10990 Ft. Caroline Road # 350352
Jacksonville, FL 32225
Visit us online: www.soaringeagleinc.org

Printed in the United States of America.

Cover photo: Micheline Chabot

GOLDEN NUGGETS
Divine Revelations

Gabriele Gilpin

Gabriele's Note

We all can learn from our experiences. The golden nuggets in this book will help you to discover God-given truth and divine revelations as you dig deep into the mysteries, all hidden within Jesus Christ. Each nugget is designed to inspire, motivate and encourage you.

Seemingly small pebbles of truth can turn into gold as we receive them and apply them to our everyday life. In my vision, I was shown pebbles in the shallow water running out of the River of Life and I was to pick up those pebbles. As I did, they actually turned into nuggets of gold! Those nuggets of gold turned out to be Words of Knowledge and Words of Wisdom.

Throughout this book you will find yourself picking up pebbles that have turned into Golden Nuggets blessing you with divine insight for situations you might be encountering.

"My sheep hear My voice." John 10:27

Every believer can receive "Heavenly Gems" and "Divine Revelations" from the Lord. If you are His sheep, then it is a fact and a promise that you can hear His voice. The only obstacles we have preventing us from receiving His word clearly, are when we do not spend time with Him. There are certain keys to hearing God's voice and those are hidden in scriptures.

One of the keys to hearing is to become still. In Habakkuk 2:1 we read: *"I will keep watch or I will listen to hear," (See Habakkuk 2:1)* which means to me, I am spending quiet time with the Lord. For some it is their prayer room, or soaking room or your favorite chair.

"Be still and know that I am God..." Psalm 46:10

"My soul waits in silence for God only." Psalm 62:1,5

Psalm 91:1 speaks of an invitation into the Secret Place. It is for us to be positioned for an encounter with God and as we draw near to God, He will draw near to us. Soaking is to become still in the presence of God and discover more about Him and to hear what He is showing and saying.

The motivation and passion behind releasing "Golden Nuggets" is Gabriele's heart desire to share with others whatever experiences she encountered in God's glory, so that they can learn and glean from her journey and to look towards a profound walk with the Father, Son and the Holy Spirit.

I pray for a fresh revelation on taking up the sword (Word of God) and what this entails for you. In His manifest Glory presence, we can hear His words of life, light, and power and follow Jesus' lead.

PROPHETIC WORDS

"I just heard the Lord speak this word for you, Gabriele: the enemy has tried to hold you back, but there is a new wind of the Spirit coming to hit your wings and take you to a new level. There is a new Scribe angel being assigned to you and you are going to write more books. The Lord is close to you and you are being invited into a deeper chamber of His presence. God is giving you a key of authority that someone had let go of in your area. You will use this key to open doorways of Heaven over people and nations."

Doug Addison
In Light Connection

"…I saw the Lord put a key into a door and opening it up. You will receive revelation keys to open up doors and after the doors are open, the glory that was inside, will come forth. He is giving you ancient keys to open up ancient places. You will go, see and perceive by the Spirit that a new realm has been released to you.
The Lord is saying that the royalty of the Holy Spirit is coming upon you and the dreams and visions you will begin to have are pure. God says to go deep in the Spirit and to write and he says when you are done writing, you are going to be changed and transformed and the books that are placed within you will be written."
Excerpt of a Prophecy given by

Bob Griffin
House of Liberty for all Nations

CONTENTS

CONTENTS CONTINUED

GOLDEN NUGGETS

After this I looked, and behold, a door standing open in heaven! And the first voice which I had heard, like the sound of a [war] trumpet speaking with me, said, "Come up here, and I will show you what must take place after these things." Revelation 4:1 AMP

One night I had an encounter and I saw an open door as an invitation to "come up". The door was wide open and there were two pillars of fire, one on the left and the other one on the right side of the door.

This door leads into the Throne Room in Heaven. Those who are born again and cleansed by the blood of the Lamb, Jesus Christ, are able to go through this door. After all, Jesus is the Door (See John 10:7).

As I entered through the door, I instinctively knew I was soaring on His sound. This sound is the song from God's heart echoing in heaven. Next I saw the fountain of living water (Revelation 7:17) and there were pebbles in the shallow part of the water.

NUGGETS OF GOLD

I knew I was to pick the pebbles up by faith…and as I did, those pebbles turned into gold. The pebbles actually turned into nuggets of gold!

After I picked them up and after they turned to gold, I also knew I had to eat them. Those nuggets of gold became pulverized in me and turned into Words of Wisdom and Words of Knowledge and Discernment. At this point I saw a minister friend of mine and we both were standing in the center of villages and towns. The people in those towns did not know what to do….but we had the words of life and we released the words of wisdom and knowledge to them, bringing relief and answers to their prayers and to their searching.

The Words of Wisdom and Words of Knowledge are two of the nine gifts of the Holy Spirit in 1 Corinthians 12. The Holy Spirit gives those gifts to whomever He wills and we can ask for those gifts to flow in us and through us. All we have to do is to yield to the Holy Spirit. I have asked for more of those words to manifest in my ministry. Many have received healing, as they acted on a Word of Knowledge to heal certain sickness.

THE WORD OF GOD LIKE A FIRE AND A HAMMER

Is not My word like fire [that consumes all that cannot endure the test]?" says the Lord, "and like a hammer that breaks the [most stubborn] rock [in pieces]? Jeremiah 23:29 AMP

God's word is like fire and He is a consuming fire. Mountains melt like wax in the presence of the Lord. The scripture I like the most can be found in Jeremiah 20:9, *"the Word of God is in my heart as a burning fire shut up in my bones."* For me this is much like what I have experienced, His words became in my heart as fire burning and overflowing my bones. Apostle Paul felt the same and said in 1 Corinthians 19:6: *"For when I preach the gospel, I cannot boast, since I am compelled to preach. Woe to me if I do not preach the gospel!"*

God's word is alive and active. Sharper than any double-edged sword, it penetrates even to dividing soul and spirit, joints and marrow; it is also like a hammer. It is pinpointing what is truly happening deep down and setting in place, restoring and renewing His intentions and exposing the enemy's schemes.

The message concerning the Word of God likened unto a Fire and a Hammer is recorded in detail in my podcast. Contact us on the website to obtain the audio teaching:

http://soaringeagleinc.org/contactandsupport.html

My prayer is that you will receive a word and golden nuggets in due season to give you direction and strength for your journey and that you will broadcast the words of life, residing in you through Jesus Christ, wherever you go.

GOLDEN NUGGETS

THE SWORD OF THE LORD AND OF GIDEON

In a vision I saw a sword lying on the ground and I heard the Lord say: "Many of my children have laid down their swords. It is time to take up the swords once again."

Immediately, I took up the sword as a prophetic act and held it towards heaven, stating that I am taking up the sword, and I am moving in the authority given to me by Jesus and I am declaring the word of the Lord over situations as the Holy Spirit leads."

This all happened right after I returned from North Africa, where one of my mandates was to declare and prophesy for the dry bones to come alive! This assignment has passed and now it was time to go forward and continue to move in the authority that has been given to me by the Lord.

Many of His children have laid down their swords! What does that mean to you? For some, it could be that, they are not taking their rightful position in the body of Christ and in His kingdom.

After praying about this vision, I heard: "the sword of the Lord and of Gideon." (See Judges 7:20) I looked up the scripture and realized how Gideon was called by God and the angel, who visited him in the winepress and called him: "Mighty man of Valor". Gideon had a hard time believing that he was a mighty man of valor. Soon, he saw God's mighty power working through just a few, only 300 of Gideon's army, who were fearless and courageous. Gideon heard someone tell a dream and through what this dream revealed, he knew God was on his side and that they would overcome the enemy. Strategies where given to him and as they followed those directions, the enemy was defeated.

THE WALL DEFENDED AGAINST THE ENEMY

Another scripture came to mind and it is in the book of Nehemiah. He was called to rebuild the wall around Jerusalem, which was not a light task. But he had a passion in his heart and he was weeping over the gross situation in Jerusalem. God was giving Nehemiah a mandate and strategies. He was anointed to discern every plot of the enemy and was not deterred from following through with the Lord's mandate. The attacks of the enemy kept coming with distractions, fear, intimidation, doubt, ridicule, confusion, scheming and conspiracy. The gift of discernment, one of the gifts of the Holy Spirit, is designed to sharpen us and to highlight what kind of spirit is operating. Nehemiah was tuned to the Lord's Spirit and detected the enemy's schemes, even when working through "friends." When facing such oppositions, we need to remember that we never fight against flesh and blood, but withstand principalities.

TAKE UP YOUR SWORD

Some, who are reading this, sense this message is for them and they know exactly what I am saying, because it resonates in their innermost being. It is time to take up your sword and use the authority that has been yours. Speak the Word of God and declare His purposes with laser-like precision and rebuke the enemy.

Now back to the book of Nehemiah. At one point the people, who helped Nehemiah rebuilding the wall, had to have a sword in one hand and worked with the other hand. This was with much determination and they were intentional about what was at hand. To be intentional about what is given to us is a mighty weapon in our arsenal. Do not give up, be vigilant and watchful instead, realizing that the enemy roams around like a roaring lion seeking whom he may devour. He comes to kill, steal and destroy, but Jesus Christ came to give us life and life more abundantly. (See John 10:10). Therefore, lift up your sword and move forward in the power of His might, clothed in the full armor of God, withstanding the fiery darts of the enemy (see Ephesians 6).

In your mind's eye try to picture, the enemy has been defeated and therefore he does not have any feet. He has been disarmed, therefore he does not have any arms and he has been defanged, therefore he does not have any teeth! What can somebody do, if they don't have any feet, or arms and are missing their teeth?

LIVING THE ELEVATED LIFE IN CHRIST

We need to be determined to continue to keep living the elevated life in Jesus Christ. In Him we live and move and have our being. He is the wall of fire around us and the glory in the midst of us. It is a fact that we are seated in heavenly places in Christ Jesus even now and every declaration, every prayer and intercession is done out of this place of authority in Him and the awareness that we can sit at the Father's table, in the midst of our enemy. He prepares a table filled with goodness and our cup is overflowing, as He anoints us with fresh oil. Receive the fresh oil and receive the overflow. Allow yourself to minister out of this overflow and see the captives go free; bondages are destroyed, because of the power that is in the blood of Jesus.

What the Lord has given you to do in this hour, is not a small thing, but of great significance. Fearlessness, determination and following through with what is given to us will cause our spiritual muscles to develop and we are encouraged to exercise our senses to discern good from evil. (See Hebrews 5:14)

Apostle Paul spoke about running the race with endurance and not boxing the air aimlessly. In Ephesians 5, we are exhorted to walk circumspectly knowing the will of the Father and therefore redeeming the time for the days are evil.

I pray for a fresh revelation on taking up the sword and what this entails for each one reading this exhortation. We need to seek the Lord in His glory, and exercise the authority given to us from the fact that we hear our Great Shepherd's voice. In His manifest presence, we can hear the words that He speaks to us with a revelation attached to it, then we can use those words of life, light and power to declare and decree. May God teach us to pray, to wait and to seek Him, so that we can agree and witness His will and His plan in our lives, because the enemy has been defeated. Therefore, we will impact the lives of others around us. You are encouraged to take up your sword and learn how to wield it skillfully. Listen to the Lord and His direction and follow His lead. Know Him intimately, know yourself and realize that you are all wrapped up in Him, and know your enemy, which means you are not ignorant of satan's devices.

JEWISH NEW YEAR 5777

The Jewish Year 5777 has been branded the year of "THE RULING SWORD". It is made up of the number 5 for grace and 3 times the number 7, which stands for the complete number of God. It is also the symbol of a fiery sword. The Bible explains, that His Word is a two edged sword, alive and active.

For the word of God is alive and active. Sharper than any double-edged sword, it penetrates even to dividing soul and spirit, joints and marrow; it judges the thoughts and attitudes of the heart. Hebrews 4:12 NIV

9

Let's get into the Word of God with a renewed vigor and ask the Holy Spirit to reveal mysteries, which are hidden in Christ Jesus. As we are filled with His living and powerful Word, and as we speak it forth, we are able to reap the harvest and see multitudes coming to Christ. The Word of God will bring us into divine alignment revealing God's purpose in our lives.

GOLDEN NUGGETS

SUPERNATURAL SIGNS AND WONDERS IN THE MIDST OF ADVERSITY

As I was praying and pondering on the raid done just in time in a suburban of Paris in 2016, I realized something very profound, faith building and inspirational and I like to share about it. Interesting enough the raid took place in Saint Denis, Northern Part of Paris, where Saint Denis was martyred.

In the third century, he was Bishop of Paris. He was martyred, with his companions Rusticus and Eleutherius, in connection with the Decian persecution of Christians, shortly after 250 AD.

Denis is said to have picked his head up after being decapitated, walked ten kilometers (six miles), while preaching a sermon of repentance the entire way.

Now this testimony might be challenging to some, but nevertheless it is an amazing account of divine intervention. Even so Denis was martyred, the Lord was not done with him and he was given supernatural power to pick up his own head and walk six miles, while preaching the Good News and repentance, the entire way! SELAH – Stop and think about it!

Every time I think about it, I picture the utter surprise of those who decapitated this man of God and thought they did their god a favor! Instead the enemy triumphing, he was made a spectacle and I can only imagine how many people bowed their knees to Jesus when they saw Saint Denis, who was the Bishop of Paris at the time, walking and preaching while holding his own head! Hallelujah!

And having spoiled principalities and powers, he made a shew of them openly, triumphing over them in it. Colossians 2:15 KJV

For this perishable must put on the imperishable, and this mortal must put on immortality. 54 But when this perishable will have put on the imperishable, and this mortal will have put on immortality, then will come about the saying that is written, "DEATH IS SWALLOWED UP in victory. 55 "O DEATH, WHERE IS YOUR VICTORY? O DEATH, WHERE IS YOUR STING?" 1 Corinthians 15:54-55NASB

The blood of the Martyrs has a voice and their sacrifice has always been the seedbed for the Church. We can expect mighty manifestations of the power of God to draw the lost and to give them a hope and a future in Him. We also know that the blood of Jesus Christ speaks a better word:

"to Jesus the mediator of a new covenant, and to the sprinkled blood that speaks a better word than the blood of Abel." Hebrews 12:24 NIV

The blood of Jesus atones us and makes possible, for Christ to dwell in us and for us in Him. It brings those who were far from God near to Him (Ephesians 2:13). It redeems us (Ephesians 1:7), and gives peace and reconciles us to God (Colossians 1:20) and so much more...

GOLDEN NUGGETS

I WILL GUIDE YOU WITH MY EYE

I will instruct you and teach you in the way you should go; I will guide you with My eye. Psalm 32:8 NKJV

I remember very well how my mother could guide me with just a look of her eyes, especially when we had company. As soon as I would start to misbehave, my mother would just glance at me and I would know, I needed to stop my behavior straight away!

When I had my boys, I trained and instructed them and they knew by my glance when they misbehaved and needed to stop. Actually, this kept all of us from much embarrassment, because I did not have to openly correct them and I was able to fine-tune the behavior and instruct them in private afterwards.

The Lord instructs and teaches me in the way I should go and He told us as parents to do the same with our children.

"Train up a child in the way he should go, and when he is old he will not depart from it." Proverbs 22:6 NKJV

My intimacy with the Lord and my willingness to receive His instructions in private will cause me to just look into His eye and understand what He is saying to me.

The scripture in Psalm 32 goes on to say: *"Do not be like the horse or like the mule, which have no understanding, which must be harnessed with bit and bridle, else they will not come near you."* *Psalm 32:9 NKJV*

Quite a few years ago, the Lord showed me, I was like a horse always running ahead of Him. What happened next was tremendous, because when I surrendered to Him, I saw myself harnessed by Him, only to have Jesus teach me as His precious and powerful war horse. Therefore, I learned how to wait upon Him and move with Him, as He desires. This is not burdensome or inhibiting, instead there is such freedom when I give Jesus the reins. Jesus knows what He placed within me and He will let me run according to His plan and purposes.

Some people are like mules, ever so stubborn, refusing to move with the Lord, and therefore always lagging behind. But there is hope for both the over-zealous horses and the stubborn mules, because Jesus will instruct us, teach us and show us the way we should go, if we so desire.

The Lord wants to guide YOU with His eye.

BREAKING OUT OF THE MOLD

"Do you not yet perceive (discern) nor understand? Are your hearts in (a settled state of) hardness?" Mark 8:17b AMPC

It is time to break out of the religious mold.

The Lord has given us spiritual eyes to see and ears to hear, to perceive and understand the sense or meaning of what He has said. Jesus asked the disciples: "Do you not yet discern nor understand? Are your hearts cold, insensitive, unfeeling and unyielding?

The reason why the disciples did not understand the meaning of what Jesus was saying to them, was because they thought only about the physical needs and things.

My cry is: *"Lord till the ground of my heart until it is ready. Remove all hardness of heart! Let me see, let me hear and discern, perceive and understand the meaning of what You are saying to me!"*

In this new season, we are given eyes and wings like the living creature in Ezekiel 1. We have eyes to see and wings to show us how to get to where we need to be.

Jesus is changing the face of the church. He has been steadily breaking down old ways and is bringing in His design, the way of the Kingdom of God. I like to watch how His children are coming out of the box of religion and bondage. It is time to move on with His ways, His direction and in His freedom.

There are many treasures within His children and they are not being released. As we continue to seek Him, to ask Him and look to Him, the Holy Spirit will give us revelation in the precious Word. After all Jesus Christ is the Living Word!

I have been witnessing how the scripture in Ephesians 4 has been highlighted in this hour. The Lord has been bringing forth His five-fold ministers, because they have been given as gifts to the Body by Jesus Christ. (See Ephesians 4:11)

His intention is to see the perfecting and the full equipping of the saints that they should do the work of ministering toward building up Christ's body. (See Ephesians 4:12)

We are to be joined together as a body working properly, so we can all grow to full maturity, all the while building each other up in love. (See Ephesians 4:16)

As this joining together takes place, everyone in the Body of Christ will be positioned and function according to God's design. Powerful, anointed and appointed teams formed by the Holy Spirit are coming together and fulfilling God's purposes.

Have you been aching for the place you can fit into, just like a puzzle piece finding its proper place?

As soon as this piece of the puzzle finds its true and appropriate place, the entire picture or puzzle becomes perfect. How good it is for brothers and sisters to dwell together in unity. There are blessings and peace provided when we are in our God-ordained place.

Doesn't it seem like there is a contradiction? I am referring to the statement, breaking out of the mold versus being placed in the puzzle? We are breaking out of the "Cookie-Cutter Christianity" mold and are positioned in a beautiful body, the Body of Christ, where there is no more bondage; only complete freedom! It is for freedom; Jesus Christ has set us free! (See Galatians 5:1)

The Lord has given us specific guidelines and directions in His word and when we are where we need to be, as with a living organism, then we are free and liberated to move with His Spirit. If you look at your body, how precisely it is fitted together and all the body parts are in perfect place, then the entire body together and united can be moved to wherever it is directed by the Holy Spirit.

GOLDEN NUGGETS

6

TRUE FREEDOM

"For the law of the Spirit of life in Christ Jesus has made me free from the law of sin and death." Romans 8:2 NKJV

The Lord has impressed on me that it seems, the hardest thing to do, is to remain free in Him. But there is a remedy for it and we can find it in Galatians 5:16 AMPC:

"But I say, walk and live (habitually) in the (Holy) Spirit (responsive to and controlled and guided by the Spirit); then you will certainly not gratify the cravings and desires of the flesh (of human nature without God)."

The practices of the flesh are listed in Galatians 5:19-21 and are in stark contrast to the fruit of the Holy Spirit listed in Galatians 5:22-23.

Where the Spirit of the Lord is there is FREEDOM! If you are thirsty for the true freedom in Christ, then remain in the Spirit of the Lord.

Decades ago, I studied in depth all about eagles and I am reminded that an eagle's cry can release another eagle, which is in captivity. The sound of the eagle, who is not in captivity, is designed to cause another eagle in depression to be set free and liberated. Therefore, it is important to stay liberated in the Spirit of the Lord and not to be entangled in man-made structures. Then we can help others to be set free by the liberating sound of heaven released through us.

"In this freedom Christ has made us free (and completely liberated us); stand fast then, and do not be hampered and held ensnared and submit again to a yoke of slavery (which you have once put off)." Galatians 5:1 AMPC

Over the past decades, I have seen many free sons and daughters of God, who have brought liberty and freedom to others, have eventually turned back to man-made structures. If you are one of those, who have tasted that freedom and liberty in the Holy Spirit, but now you have come under this yoke of slavery again, then turn to the Lord, humble yourself and be released once again. As you repent and return to your *first love* and do the former things, you shall be restored. (Revelations 2:4-5)

Many, who have begun their new spiritual life and have walked by the Holy Spirit, have been deceived and tried to reach perfection by depending on the carnal nature instead of continuing to flow and yield to the Holy Spirit. As Apostle Paul pointed out to the Galatians:

"Why are you trying to finish in the flesh, what was started in the Spirit?

"Are you so foolish and so senseless and so silly? Having begun (your new life spiritually) with the (Holy) Spirit, are you now reaching perfection (by dependence) on the flesh?" Galatians 3:3 AMPC

The Life in the Spirit shatters the work of the enemy, who attempts to hold you back from reaching your full potential and tries to entangle and enslave you. Actually, his plans are destroyed as you embrace the assignments of the Kingdom of Heaven. Ask the Lord to unveil your assignments and then capture them and walk the pre-ordained mission out.

You are His beloved and are well able to rely on His triumphing voice. He made provisions for you to be liberated and to be released from the shackles of tradition and man-made structures. His Liberty, Life and Love is flowing through your veins and being, because you are One with Christ.

The Lord is saying: *"Don't let anything hold you back from Me, hear Me as I am calling you."*

In the book of Genesis, Pharaoh tried to keep the children of God from worshipping freely and to taste the release from slavery. Thus God had Moses declare:

"LET MY PEOPLE GO!

There is provision made to be free to dance, to sing, and to worship Him in Spirit and Truth!

GOLDEN NUGGETS

7

TREASURES AND HIDDEN RICHES

"And I will give you the treasures of darkness and hidden riches of secret places, that you may know that it is I, the Lord, the God of Israel, Who calls you by your name." Isaiah 45:3 NKJV

I have heard of many instances, where treasures have been found in unusual and secret places. For example, a couple moved into a new home and found over $10.000 in the freezer wrapped in a plastic bag and aluminum foil. At first they thought it was old meat and almost threw it away, but when they investigated, they saw it was money rolled up.

A contractor found a large amount of money hidden in a wall, he tore down. Another man found a gem in his back yard and I heard of several Christians, who have been blessed by the Lord with gems and precious stones. Many treasures are still to be found on the bottom of the ocean, as well as all over the earth.

We can look at riches in currency or riches of this world, but in the body of Christ we have a more precious treasure in who, everything we ever need, is wrapped up.

"For it is the God Who commanded light to shine out of darkness, who has shone in our hearts to give the light of the knowledge of the glory of God in the face of Jesus Christ. But we have this precious treasure in earthen vessels, that the excellence of the power may be of God and not of us." 2 Corinthians 4:6, 7 NKJV

Jesus in us is that precious treasure and our inward man is being renewed day by day. Our momentary light affliction is working for us a far more exceeding and eternal weight of glory. We don't look at the things which are seen, for they are only temporal, but at the things which are not seen, for they are eternal (See 2 Corinthians 4:16-18).

I know the Lord is giving us treasures and hidden riches to further the kingdom of God, but this is not to be our main focus. As we seek His kingdom and His righteousness first, all these things, the people in this world are trying to obtain will be added to us.

Paul states in Philippians 2:20-22 that he has no one like-minded, who will sincerely care for the state of them. For all seek their own and not the things which are of Christ Jesus.

Let us not be caught up with seeking our own, but seeking the things which are of Christ Jesus. Even Peter was rebuked by Jesus when he tried to correct and stop Him from going to the cross.

"But He turned and said to Peter, "Get behind Me, Satan! You are an offense to Me, for you are not mindful of the things of God, but the things of men. Then Jesus said to His disciples, "If anyone desires to come after Me, let him deny himself, and take up his cross, and follow Me. For whoever desires to save his life will lose it, but whoever loses his life for My sake will find it." Matthew 16:23-25 NKJV

My deepest desire is to follow Jesus and to lose my life for His sake. How about you? This decision will take us on an amazing and delightful journey with Jesus. After all in losing my life for His sake, I will actually find it and I will be given His abundant life. Oh, how precious is He and how remarkable are His ways. He holds the keys to life and death.

The Lord taught us to pray and to ask for the Father's kingdom to come and for His will to be done. We are also taught in Proverbs 13:22 NLT

"Good people leave an inheritance to their grandchildren, but the sinner's wealth passes to the godly."

These are wonderful promises and I am especially excited about leaving an inheritance not just to my children, but also for my grandchildren. The sinner's wealth will be passed on to the godly people. It is a privilege and in order to receive it, I need not to fall for temptation and therefore I should be mindful to guard my heart with all diligence. After all out of my heart flows the wellspring of life. (See Proverbs 4:23)

"If I desire to be rich I can fall into temptation and a snare, and into many foolish and harmful lusts which drown men in destruction and perdition. For the love of money is a root of all kinds of evil, for which some have strayed from the faith in their greediness; and pierced themselves through with many sorrows. But you, O man of God, flee these things and pursue righteousness, godliness, faith, love, patience, gentleness. Fight the good fight of faith..." (See 1 Timothy 6:9-12a)

As most of you know, I travel to various nations and every time I return, I sense the principality of greed that seems to be upon this nation. Many chase the "American dream" and honestly I wonder, what is this dream all about? It has been infiltrated into a majority of the body of Christ. This is not to point the fingers towards anyone in particular, because we do not fight against flesh and blood, but against the principalities and rulers in heavenly places.

I can actually sense "this pressure to produce" and it is often masked by saying we need to produce for the sake of the kingdom. This seems to be such a noble thing to do! But what is the underlying motive? This is why it is extremely important to have a pure heart and clean hands, which is possible in Christ Jesus. His blood has purified us and as we walk in Him, and as we are aware of our position in Him, our innermost being will desire to soar above all these hindrances and remain in the High Places in and with Him.

The Lord's promises and blessing are real and I have been hearing the following two words for this season,

ABUNDANCE AND OVERFLOW

We will see abundance and overflow coming to His children. The Lord has been testing our hearts to see if we will remain true to Him, when He starts releasing the fullness of these blessings.

Much shaking has been going on, especially in the arena of finances. Why? Because He loves us so much and desires for us to be prepared to receive this abundance and overflow, without the love for money, which is the root of all evil. It is not the money that is the root of all evil, but the love of money. Money is a tool in our hands to glorify God and we can give lavishly and freely, as we have been given.

He desires a devoted heart of love for Him and for His kingdom first and foremost. In order to sincerely care for His children and to have a proven character, just as Timothy did, as we see Paul remarking:

"As a son with his father he served with me in the gospel, not seeking his own, but the things which are of Christ Jesus, (See Philippians 2:21-22)

May this season bless you with abundance and overflow!

GOLDEN NUGGETS

8

SEVEN PILLARS OF WISDOM

Wisdom has built her house; she has set up its seven pillars. 2 She has prepared her meat and mixed her wine she has also set her table. 3 She has sent out her servants, and she calls from the highest point of the city, 4 "Let all who are simple come to my house!" To those who have no sense she says, 5 "Come, eat my food and drink the wine I have mixed. 6 Leave your simple ways and you will live; walk in the way of insight." Proverbs 9:1-6 NIV

Wisdom has built a great house on seven pillars and they represent seven principals for success.

This Proverb has been taught many different ways and the ones I have heard, have all been with much insight to glean from. In this book, I like to share what insight I have received at 3 o'clock on an early summer morning.

When I read Proverbs 9:1-6, all of a sudden I was enlightened and saw an outline on how to develop a business or ministry plan. This outline can also be used to prepare for special events, meetings and conferences.

Before I founded Soaring Eagle Ministries in 1996, I was given a vision by the Lord. One of my emphases is to teach about how important it is to have a God-given vision. In the first book of the series 'Soaring Eagle School of the Spirit' (see page 126), I added a chapter focusing on 'vision casting' and how to receive clear purpose and direction from the Lord, all according to Habakkuk 2:2.

"Record the vision and inscribe it on tablets, that the one who reads it may run. " Habakkuk 2:2

- ➢ Receiving the vision from the Father
- ➢ Write the vision and publish it
- ➢ Praying the vision
- ➢ Sharing the vision

My prayer is that God will give you a fresh download of His will and purposes for your life. It is true, when you receive direction from the Lord, it can give you clarity and resolve for years to come. Along with the revelation of the Father's will comes responsibility. When the Lord shows us His purpose, it is so that we can make preparations toward it.

THE SEVEN PILLARS OF LEADERSHIP WISDOM

Let's look at Proverbs 9:1-6 a bit closer, because here I found my outline of the seven pillars. As an example, in the following outline, I am focusing on how to prepare for an upcoming dinner event.

i. PREPARING
1b She has set up its seven pillars
2a She has prepared her meat and mixed her wine
She has a plan and she is in the preparation mode

ii. ORGANIZING
2b She has also set her table
She is organizing and setting up the meeting place

iii. DELEGATING
3a She has sent out her servants
She delegates wisely and knows her team well

iv. ADVERTISING
3b She calls from the highest point of the city
She strategically advertises and makes sure everyone hears about it

v. INVITING
4 Let all who are simple come to my house!" To those who have no sense she says,
5 Come, eat my food and drink the wine I have mixed.
She targets certain people and then offers solutions, help and guidance to those who are in need

vi. EQUIPPING
6a Leave your simple ways and you will live
Wisdom equips the leaders and manages the growth

vii. LEADERSHIP TRAINING
6b Walk in the way of insight
The team is trained with insight and guidelines, with a team mentality designed for multiplication

The wisdom of God is supreme and these seven pillars of preparing, organizing, delegating, advertising, inviting, equipping and leadership training is all we need to launch a fruitful event, seminar, conference, wedding or business meeting.

Before organizing an event, I have learned to categorize everything under the seven headings. Then I pray for strategies and how to fill in the puzzle pieces. Decisions are made, such as what is needed in supplies and manpower to prepare, where will the event be held, how many helpers do I need, what is the best way to advertise, who do I invite, and who is my team of leaders in need of being equipped and trained.

These are very effective and proven keys for a project you may want to undertake, any organization you like to lead, and any new ministry you may want to birth.

GOLDEN NUGGETS

9

GODLINESS WITH CONTENTMENT IS GREAT GAIN

"Now godliness with contentment is great gain."
1 Timothy 6:6

One morning during prayer I heard the word: "discontentment." This caused me to search out the topic in the Bible, especially since I like to be content in the Lord and I want to avoid the hazards of discontentment. During my research, I discovered that *contentment* has to be learned and developed.

The Apostle Paul stated in *Philippians 4:11 NKJV* *"Not that I speak in regard to need, for I have learned in whatever state I am, to be content."*

Paul walked through many issues and even difficult situations in his life and through it; he learned how to be content. He knew how to be fulfilled no matter where he was in life; in living humbly or living in prosperity. He realized that he was able to do anything through Christ, who gave him strength. His source was Jesus, not his circumstances. Paul knew if he was to grumble, fault find, or allowed discouragement to settle in, he would not be able to reach for and enjoy the Father's abundance and the riches of the heavenly realm. Paul was determined to finish his race and he kept the faith and it did not matter to him what he had to do or where he had to go, because he learned his lessons and his character was developed in the midst of his circumstances.

MANY ARE INCREASINGLY DISCONTENT

Many believe that money and health are the answer to discontentment. However, the constant search and thriving to be more, to do more and to chase a "better tomorrow", instead of enjoying God's blessings right where we are, has left many empty and discouraged.

DISCONTENTMENT COMES WHEN WE FOCUS ONLY ON WHAT WE DON'T HAVE

A posture of being thankful in what we do have, leads to contentment and a joyful state.

The Lord does not require for us to be without ambitions, visions and goals, but He warns us from focusing only on what we are lacking. After all He said that He would NEVER LEAVE US NOR FORSAKE US. In Him we move and live and have our being and in Him we have everything we ever need.

"Let your conduct be without covetousness; be content with such things as you have, for He Himself has said, "I will never leave you nor forsake you." So we may boldly say: "The Lord is my helper; I will not fear, what man can do to me?" Hebrews 13:5, 6 NKJV

He promised that we will have all that we need in every circumstance and that we will have an abundance and overflow for and in every good work (see 2 Corinthians 9:8). Isn't that amazing!?

This state of godliness with contentment is great gain to us, because it is like dew from heaven and I see it as raindrops bringing refreshing in a dry and thirsty land. I bless you to fly as an eagle, soaring high and liberated from all worldly desires and any fear. I bless you in the name of Jesus, in whom there is liberty! Do not forget to enjoy your life this very moment and be thankful for what you already have.

GOLDEN NUGGETS

10

RUNNING THE RACE WITH ENDURANCE

During a time of devotion I was prompted to read Psalm 116:7 and the part about: "Return to your rest, O my soul," was highlighted to me. David knew what to do when he left the *Rest of God* and told his soul to return to its rest. We are in need to learn how to rest in the Lord!

Further down in verse 13, I read: "I will take up the cup of salvation". I asked the Lord to show me what it really means to partake of the cup of salvation! Soon I was in the middle of a vision.

In this vision Jesus stood in front of me with the cup of salvation in His right hand. We were in the Garden under an apple tree and I was gazing at His wonderful, awe-inspiring face. His eyes sparkled with delight and He had a huge smile on His face.

Jesus was dressed in a flowing garment like He wore while living on earth. Then He took the cup, placed it on my lips and gave me a drink from the cup of salvation. The drink felt like a warm, yet refreshing sip, much like a heavy red wine with a taste of citrus and an undertone of woodsy substance. Now, when you drink something, say a glass of water, and you empty it, you ingest it, you internalize it and it becomes part of you. This drink went throughout my entire body; every part of my body was affected, even all the way down into my toes! It was electrifying and filled with destiny, yet full of His abundant Life. Then Jesus took my right hand and we began to run through the fields and soon we followed a fresh path. The path was not there before, but appeared as we kept running. A new path of destiny was unfolding!

Soon, while still running next to Him, I felt like I was pulled into Jesus' body and we were one. I was abiding in Him and He was abiding in me. (See John 15)

During this experience, I kept running next to Him, but was aware that actually I was in Him and He was in me – intertwined and in harmony with the Father's will and purpose. The cup of salvation was available to me, because of the cup Jesus drank in the Garden of Gethsemane.

There He spoke words of surrender, while in the Garden, hours before the cross. There He saw the cup that the Father had extended to Him, a cup that He must drink. Jesus asked if this cup could be removed from Him. Nevertheless, Jesus yielded to the Father's plan and design. He drank the cup and suffered, was crucified and rose again from the dead. He overcame the world system, death and the devil's schemes (See Matthew 26:42, John 18:11).

JESUS IS OUR CUP OF SALVATION

We drink His blood and agree with the Father's will, as we fully surrender and become ONE with Him and the Father by faith.

I have been crucified with Christ and I no longer live, but Christ lives in me. The life I now live in the body, I live by faith in the Son of God, who loved me and gave himself for me. Galatians 2:20 NIV

Our soul finds rest alone in Him and Jesus is the Restorer of the soul! Salvation was purchased by Jesus in full and it is SOZO in Greek (see Romans 10:9). In the Strong's Concordance "SOZO" means "to save, deliver, protect, heal, preserve, do well, and be made whole." Very clearly we see that it includes salvation, deliverance, protection, healing, prospering and being made whole.

WHY WERE WE CONTINUALLY RUNNING?

Back to my vision, I wondered why we continued to run in the vision and Jesus spoke through Paul: "*since we have so great a cloud of witnesses surrounding us, let us also lay aside every encumbrance and the sin which so easily entangles us, and let us run with endurance the race that is set before us, fixing our eyes on Jesus, the author and finisher of faith.*"*(See Hebrews 12:1-2)*

Let's shake off any entanglements and forsake every sin trying to prevent us from running the race with endurance and staying aglow and burning in the Spirit.

41

GOLDEN NUGGETS

11

IN MY FATHER'S HOUSE

"In My Father's House are many rooms; if it were not so, I would have told you. I am going there to prepare a place for you." John 14:2 NIV

Let me share a vision I had. In it I was standing in a very long hallway in My Father's house in heaven. In the scripture above, Jesus tells us about the many rooms in His Father's house. If there are rooms as Jesus tells us, then I assume and it is only logical, that there will be at least one hallway or even more than just one hallway.

In any case, as I walked down the hallway, I noticed what looked like large pictures on the walls to the left and to the right. This stirred up my curiosity and I stood in front of one of those pictures. As I stood there gazing at the picture frame, suddenly the picture turned into something like a plasma TV and a movie started to play. I watched for a moment and realized it was a scene or event out of the Bible. Actually it was not just a movie; it felt like I was a part of it all. Right in front of me I watched what Paul did in Ephesus when he was escorted to the theater. I did not only watch it, but it was as if I was a part of it and knew supernaturally everything about it. I had an understanding of the culture and the sayings and gestures of people. It was all very familiar and what was happening made complete sense to me.

I even sensed what the people in this event were feeling and I knew what they were thinking and the intentions of their hearts. The Lord is laying bare the thoughts and intentions of the heart of people. In the heavenly realm all can be seen, because the light of the Lord is making manifest the hidden things. Even here on earth, darkness cannot hide in the presence and glory of the Lord.

When I was done watching the scene in the picture in front of me, I moved to the next frame and the same thing happened there, except it was another event in the Bible. I was astounded and delighted about the wisdom, knowledge and understanding of the event I saw, because of the perfect revelation given by the Holy Spirit. This is exactly what already belongs to us. We can ask for God's wisdom and insight and it will be freely given to us, even while we are still in this earthly tent, which I like to call my earth-suit. After all we already live in eternity and we are seated in Christ Jesus in heavenly places right now. Our divine position is not to try to gain something up there, but to embrace what we have already been given and what is part of our divine birthright in the Spirit of God.

The Bible truly came alive during this vision and I like to visit this hallway in the Spirit of God very often. This encounter seemed to me like visiting the "hall of fame (faith)", and it reminds me of the faith chapter in Hebrews 11. In it we can enjoy the manifold testimonies of those who went before us and walked by faith in the Son of God.

Even now as I read the word of God and meditate on it and the events, I find myself being part of it and suddenly I understand and receive revelation. This adds to my faith walk and I can literally see myself doing great exploits for my God, because I know Him and my eyes, ears and understanding are opened up to the realm of His glory.

GOLDEN NUGGETS

12

A MERRY HEART

Therefore the king said to me, "Why is your face sad, since you are not sick? This is nothing but sorrow of heart." Nehemiah 2:2 NKJV

This pagan king Artaxerxes discerned that Nehemiah had sorrow of heart and granted him to return to Jerusalem, and he was willing to help him in order to fulfill God's perfect will.

In this writing, I like to focus on having a merry heart instead of walking with sorrow in the heart. Of course, there are times of intercession where we feel the sadness and are broken before the Lord and this is a good thing. Those who are familiar with intercession know that as we intercede and the burden lifts, we can actually feel the pleasure of God and a release. With it comes a sense of accomplishment, because there has been a co-laboring with Christ in prayer, intercession and the spirit of supplication.

On the contrary, when I consistently feel sad, or feel afraid without any reason, or if I have a nagging feeling of "something is wrong" and there is not a prayer burden, then I need to be aware of the guilt and condemnation and even the anxiety, which is trying to overwhelm me.

Let's focus on the following scriptures to find our answers.

"A merry heart does good, like medicine, But a broken spirit dries the bones." Proverbs 17:22

"A merry heart makes a cheerful countenance, but by sorrow of the heart the spirit is broken." Proverbs 15:13

"But he who is of a merry heart has a continual feast." Proverbs 15:15b

"Rejoice in the Lord always and again I say rejoice" Philippians 4:4 KJV

"Rejoice always." 1 Thessalonians 5:16

Recently I took on some burdens that are not mine and the Lord woke me at 3 o'clock one night and gave me this message on a merry heart. If I have a merry heart, I will have a continual feast! I will be continually rejoicing in the Lord, giving Him thanks in everything and keeping my heart pure. This feast is actually about "taste and see that the Lord is good."

When we are full of joy, our minds, bodies and spirits are affected by it. Your mind can sense true joy which helps the immune system and it is medicinal.

If you are plagued by fear, worry, stress, depression and anger, you are opening the door to sickness. Your body is not secreting what it requires to keep you healthy and it is a set-up for failure. Turn from it quickly!

"Anxiety in the heart of man causes depression, but a good word makes it glad." Proverbs 12:25 NKJV

We are designed to give good words, words of exhortation, even a word in season to him who is weary. As the Lord is awakening us each morning, our ears hear words of wisdom and words of knowledge to give to others in need.

"The Lord God has given me the tongue of the learned, that I should know how to speak, a word in season to him who is weary. He awakens me morning by morning. He awakens my ear to hear as the learned." Isaiah 50:4 NKJV

How important it is to have an ear that is in tune to hear what the Lord is saying and then to be able to take these words and use them to refresh others, who are weary, full of anxiety and depressed.

A Merry and Joyful Heart is like medicine!

GOLDEN NUGGETS

13

GOD'S GRACE IS SUFFICIENT

In the early morning hours of a day in autumn, I was awoken by a phone call from a family member and the news was not pleasant. After the phone call I prayed again and suddenly I felt this amazing presence and I asked the Lord what it was.

It was the grace of God.

Now you may say how can you feel the grace of God? Well, how can you feel the presence of God, or the love of God? I was crying tears of joy, because it was a heavy glory cloud and I was undone realizing again that apart from Jesus I can do nothing (see John 15).

At the same time numerous scriptures came to my mind, all at the same time, so it seemed.

One of them was 2 Corinthians 12:9a. In this scripture, Paul shared about his encounter with the grace of God. He asked the Lord three times to remove the thorn in his flesh, which was a messenger of satan to buffet him, lest he was exalted above measure. (See 2 Corinthians 12:7, 8)

"And He said to me, "My grace is sufficient for you, for My strength is made perfect in your weakness."

The tune of the song: "Amazing Grace" played in my mind and since I watched the movie, I was able to further understand the grace, the author wrote about.

During this time, the Tropical Storm Hanna swirled around the east coast of the USA. Shortly thereafter, I found out that Hanna is a Hebrew name for grace! The Lord is speaking with His grace. He gives grace to the humble, but He resists the proud and He raises up the humble in His timing.

I believe we are living in a crucial time for all of us and we must know that the grace of God is still sufficient. As it was for Paul so many centuries ago, so it is still available to us now.

When you know you can't change a situation and only God can, then remember the grace of God is still sufficient. You will be able to face the "storms" of life relying heavily on the grace of God and by casting your cares upon Him, because He cares about you and everything that pertains to you.

And as He said in Zechariah 4:6b - 7 NKJV "Not by might, nor by power, but by My Spirit, says the Lord of hosts. Who are you, "O great mountain? Before Zerubbabel you shall become a plain! And he shall bring forth the capstone with shouts of "Grace, grace to it!"

I know I can't do anything in my own might or strength, but by the Holy Spirit this mountain of obstacle will become a plain. The capstone is nothing less than the chief cornerstone, Jesus Christ. (See Psalm 118:22, Acts 4:11). When sin abounds, grace much more abounds. In the midst of chaos, Paul learned that God's grace was sufficient. Jesus has not changed a matter of fact, He is the same yesterday, today and forever, therefore His grace is still sufficient.

Who are you? Who is this great mountain?

What are your mountains of obstacles?

Speak grace to the mountains of obstacles and observe how Jesus Christ will arise in the midst of the situation.

During the recent threat of nuclear bombing by North Korea, I asked the Lord how to intercede? He reminded me of the scripture in Zechariah 4 and I declared: "Grace, Grace, Grace to this mountain of obstacles."

GRACE GIVEN

Those who are humble are given much grace in this hour, but those who are full of pride will be resisted and brought low for a time. There has been much sifting in the Body of Christ and it is time to let go of all the weight and the sin that so easily entangles us.

It is by the mercies of God that we are able to present our bodies as a living sacrifice, holy and acceptable to the Lord, which is our reasonable service.

GOLDEN NUGGETS

14

WAIT AND LISTEN AND COME TO THE WATERS

Wait and listen, everyone who is thirsty! Come to the waters; and he who has no money, come, buy and eat! Yes, come, buy [priceless, spiritual] wine and milk without money and without price [simply for the self-surrender that accepts the blessing]. Isaiah 55:1 AMPC

I was asked a question: "What do you think is in the way and what are your limitations as far as moving forward in and with the Lord?"

The Lord's answer to this question, as I asked Him, was short and to the point: "You are!"

You know I always say, if there is a problem it stems from me not from the Lord. Evidently, this is the case again! The scripture that came immediately into my mind was Isaiah 55:1 in the Amplified version. Did I really need amplification??!!

In this version of the Bible, the last part of verse one sticks out: "Simply for the self-surrender that accepts the blessing."

This showed me and confirmed that I was in God's way. My own thoughts and ideas are in the way, because His thoughts and His ways are higher than mine. My mind is in need of being renewed daily by the word of God. So, during a worship time I saw myself being decapitated and my head was rolling on the floor! Wow, what a picture...Lord, what are You saying? Simply this vision was telling me, that He needs to be the head and I need to follow Him and not the other way around. After all, Jesus is the Head of the Body of Christ!

Suddenly I was aware of my need to surrender and come to Him to receive without cost. He is the fountain of living waters and I can freely receive from Him the nourishment I need. As I yield to Him, I can drink the spiritual wine and I am conscious of my need of it, because by it my soul is refreshed, supported and strengthened. This includes releasing my worries, anxieties and limitations into His hands, as I humble myself under the mighty hand of God. I am even more aware of the fact, that I can give Him all of my cares, because He lovingly cares for me. (See 1 Peter 5:6, 7)

Jesus came to set me free, so I can live in the supernatural realm, in the realm of the Father's glory. In His presence is fullness of joy and in His realm, the heavenly realm, there is no lack, no poverty, no sickness, and no disease. *No dis-ease!*

With God all things are possible and there aren't any limitations in Him.

And He [further] said to me, it is done! I am the Alpha and the Omega, the Beginning and the End. To the thirsty I [Myself] will give water without price from the fountain (springs) of the water of Life. Revelation 21:6

The [Holy] Spirit and the bride (the church, the true Christians) say, Come! And let him who is listening say, Come! And let everyone come who is thirsty [who is painfully conscious of his need of those things by which the soul is refreshed, supported, and strengthened]; and whoever [earnestly] desires to do it, let him come, take, appropriate, and drink the water of Life without cost. Revelation 22:17AMPC

Lord I come and partake and receive this water of Life. I allow it to go deeply into the bottom of my soul and to saturate my entire being. I desire to be saturated in Your Presence, to remain in Your glory presence and being guided by Your presence, as I am transformed into Your brilliant image.

Lord, I surrender and give up trying to do it my way or the way of the world. I will WAIT and LISTEN and come to drink and eat from your blessings.

The deer that pants for the water brook is thirsty and desperate for the refreshing drink. The River of Life, already within us, is flowing out of me and a constant overflow of this water is refreshing my soul and others around me.

What is in the way, or what are your limitations preventing you from coming to His River of Life?

GOLDEN NUGGETS

15

DIVINE REVELATIONS AND HEAVENLY GEMS

"My sheep hear My voice." John 10:27 KJV

Every believer can receive "Heavenly Gems" and "Divine Revelations" from the Lord. If you are His sheep, then it is a fact and a promise that you can hear His voice. The only obstacles we have preventing us from receiving His word clearly, are when we do not spend time with Him. There are certain keys to hearing God's voice and those are hidden in scriptures.

PERSONAL APPLICATION

Our goal should be to "Delight in the Father of Glory", to learn more about Him, to dive into His mysteries and to apply the truth revealed to us. Personal application is at the very heart of discipleship and spiritual growth.

Receive the "good news" of God's kingdom and enjoy the journey with Him, imitating the Father and remaining in Christ Jesus. Jesus said in John 6:63: *"It is the Spirit who gives life; the flesh profits nothing. The words that I speak to you are spirit, and they are life."*

One of the keys to hearing the God of the Scriptures is to become still. In Habakkuk 2:1 we read: *"I will stand at my guard post..,"* which means to me, I am spending quiet time with the Lord in silence. For some it is their prayer room, or soaking room or your favorite chair. Soaking is to become still in the presence of God and discover more about the Father, the Son and the Holy Spirit. (See *Psalm 46:10, Psalm 62:1,5)* Psalm 91:1 speaks of an invitation into the Secret Place. It is to be positioned for an encounter with God and as we draw near to God, He will draw near to us.

REVELATIONS AND GEMS

"I will keep watch or I will listen to hear." *(See Habakkuk 2:1)*

As we become still before the Lord, we will become more acquainted. Out of that time of fixing our eyes on Jesus, we will be able to see visions, hear and perceive what He is saying to us. These revelations and gems can include words of wisdom and knowledge, as released by the Spirit of God. Many times during soaking, I hear God telling me about my next assignment or I see people and nations in front of my eyes. Often He gives me scriptures to confirm what He is saying, so that I can then move into a revelatory assignment.

FOCUS ON THE HEAVENLY REALM

In a vision I was taken into the Treasure Room in heaven. Yes, there is such a room and it is an impressive place. There three ancient keys were handed to me and I was shown three treasure chests. Each chest had a golden lock. I took one of the keys and it fit perfectly into the lock of the first chest. With a turn of the key it was opened. This chest represented all the generational inheritance from my earthly Father's side. I saw all of the promises, callings and blessings, which are supposed to be fulfilled by my ancestors, but somehow had never been walked out. I was compelled to declare and call forth each promise as I prophetically pulled them out of the chest: "I declare that the calling on my ancestors are being released to my generation and to the generations to come. All the wealth, provisions and health are restored now. Divine opportunities and assignments are taken back and will be manifesting again in Jesus' Name."

While I was declaring and decreeing, it felt like I was wielding a mighty, ancient, golden sword. This sword was piercing the darkness and all the destinies and promises were unleashed.

Now it was time to pay attention to the next treasure chest. The second key fit perfectly, just as the first one did. This one unveiled and represented all the generational inheritance from my earthly Mother's side and I sensed I needed to use the same ancient sword again. Therefore, I started to call forth promises, blessings, missed opportunities, divine appointments and assignments as well as creativity. As I decreed and declared the word of the Lord and for the divine will, elections and destinies to be released into my generation now, I felt a Holy Spirit charge and an empowering on what was happening and how amazing, breathtaking and astounding this experience was.

The third treasure chest was opened the same way as the previous two. But before I opened it, I was wondering what could this possibly mean? By now I understood that the first two chests contained destinies from my ancestors, but I could not imagine what treasures are hidden in the third one. To my surprise the chest was filled with creative ideas, witty inventions, missed callings and even more God-given strategies. I really thrive on strategic planning and enjoy receiving it from the Lord and walking them out.

Once more I was wielding this sword and declaring and decreeing, calling those things that are not as if they were. Bringing those blessings into the now and asking like *David did: "O Lord, the word which you have spoken concerning Your servant and his house, let it be established forever."*

This experience was a definite marker of breakthrough and following are some examples from the Bible for what happened to me.

1 Chronicles 17:23-24a
And now, O Lord, the word which You have spoken concerning Your servant and concerning his house, let it be established forever, and do as You have said. 24 So let it be established, that Your name may be magnified forever.

As new covenant believers, we have been given access to the throne of grace, and have been told we can come boldly before that third heaven throne room to obtain mercy and grace. (Hebrews 4:16)

16

GOD'S PRESENCE

In 1 Samuel 5 we read about the Ark of the Covenant, being taken by the Philistines to the house of Dagon and set next to the idol.

The house of Dagon represented temples, which were erected in honor of this idol and was the principal deity of the Philistines. It looked like a combination of a human head, breast, and arms, joined to the belly and had a tail of a fish. The captured Ark of the Covenant was placed in the temple of Dagon, right in front of this demonic image.

What happened next is amazing. During the night, the idol fell on its face before the presence of God. Although set up, it fell again and lay in a state of complete mutilation; its head and arms, severed from the trunk, were lying in distant and separate places, as if violently cast off, and only the fishy part remained. The degradation of the Philistines' idol was now even more noticeable. Its surmise declared the superiority of the God of Israel.

The only Head of the church, which is the body of Christ, is Jesus Christ.

"And He put all things under His feet, and gave Him to be head over all things to the church, which is His body, the fullness of Him who fills all in all." Ephesians 1:22, 23 NKJV

As outlined in Ephesians 4, Jesus gave us gifts and released the five-fold ministers; Apostles, Prophets, Pastors, Teachers and Evangelists. They are to train, equip and release the saints to do the work of the ministry. The head above them all is Jesus. Even the gifts of the Holy Spirit are given as the Spirit wills.

"But one and the same Spirit works all these things, distributing to each one individually, as He wills." 1 Corinthians 12:11 NKJV

We need to be fitly joined to Jesus, as an individual and then properly joined to the Body of Christ to function in our appointed places. We are called "Living Stones" chosen by God and precious, and are being built up a "Spiritual House." (See 1 Peter 2:4, 5)

As we submit one to another in the Body of Christ, loving and preferring one another, God's spiritual house, where His presence dwells, will be developed.

As Paul said "follow me as I follow Christ," I am realizing how often people have followed "heads" of ministries and churches without a personal relationship and thought they are fulfilling God's purpose. Instead we are to follow Christ and receive teaching and instructions from leaders, with whom we have been divinely joined together in love forming close-knit relationships, *in order for all of us to grow up in all things into Him who is the head - Christ - from whom the whole body, joined and knit together by what every joint supplies, according to the effective working by which every part does its share, causes growth of the body for the edifying of itself in love. (See Ephesians 4:15, 16)*

The Body of Christ is not an organization, but a living organic expression of His heart and must have the love and life of God flowing through it.

The Seven Spirits of God (Wisdom, Understanding, Counsel, Might, Knowledge, and the Fear of the Lord and the Spirit of the Lord) are sent by the Father to teach us, so that we grow into maturity and to show us the protocol of His kingdom (See Isaiah 11:1-2)

As sons of God, born again of His incorruptible seed, (See 1 Peter 1:23), we are given maturity appropriate freedom without manipulation. Therefore, let's not bow down to idols, but worship God, the Father, Son and Holy Spirit. If need be return to your first love! Let's not idolize shining gifts in the body of Christ or elevate anyone or anything above Jesus.

"Blessing and honor and glory and power be to Him who sits upon the throne and unto the Lamb, forever and ever!" Revelations 5:13b NKJV

GOLDEN NUGGETS

17

WONDERS IN THE HEAVENS AND SIGNS ON THE EARTH

I will show wonders in the heavens above and signs on the earth below, blood and fire and billows of smoke. [20] The sun will be turned to darkness and the moon to blood before the coming of the great and glorious day of the Lord. [21] And everyone who calls on the name of the Lord will be saved. Acts 2:19-21 NKJV

Years ago when I lived in New Jersey, I flew often to Houston, Texas to minister and my youngest son Steven would come with me.

On one such occasion, as we embarked on the flight to Newark, NJ, Steven kept saying that we are going to fly into New York. I thought he confused New York with Newark and corrected him, that we were flying to Newark NOT New York. But he insisted on what he originally said. So I just left it alone.

After we had flown awhile and came towards the end of the flight, the captain of the airplane announced that the brakes on the airplane are malfunctioning and we would fly into JFK, New York instead of landing in Newark, N.J. The reason why we were heading towards JFK was because the runway was longer, than the one in Newark. Well, I guess the prophetic gift in my son was once again extremely accurate.

When we heard this challenging announcement, I started praying immediately about this situation. Back then I called this kind of intercession "emergency tongues".

In the early night hours, the approach into JFK was in progress and the sky was dark. As I looked out of the airplane window I spotted the moon. Would you believe it, it was blood red! Immediately I was reminded of the scripture in Acts 2:19-21, were Peter was quoting Joel's prophecy. The Lord will show wonders in the heavens above and signs on the earth below....the moon shall be turned into blood.....and it shall come to pass, that whoever calls on the name of the Lord shall be saved.

Out of my mouth, I started proclaiming the word of the Lord and told the passengers around me about this prophecy. I asked the passenger next to me, do you know where you are heading, in the event something would happen and that he had an opportunity to receive Jesus as his Lord and Savior right now.

All in all this was a great opportunity to witness, because I had their undivided attention. Not only was the word proclaimed, but the brakes on the airplane worked fine. The emergency crew stood by for nothing …..Thankfully!

Why am I sharing this tidbit? It is because we will see signs and wonders, even wonders in heaven above and signs in the earth beneath. God is revealing Himself in extra-ordinary ways and the knowledge of His glory shall be seen all over the earth, as the waters in the sea.

It is very important to recognize the gifts and calling in our children. We are their parent and God has chosen us to steward those precious ones. Ask the Lord to reveal it, so you can train up your child and make way for the gifts. It is a fact that they will receive the same gift of the Holy Spirit, as you have and they seem to be more in tune with the heavenly realm than some adults. I know my children move in prophecy, words of wisdom and knowledge and I do listen to what the Spirit is saying through them.

You will receive the gift of the Holy Spirit. This promise is for you. It is also for your children. (See Acts 2:38, 39)

When we know what the talents and gifts of our children are, then we can make room for them and watch them flourish right before our eyes.

It is time to stir up and to fan to flames the gifts within our children and others around us.

GOLDEN NUGGETS

PERSERVERANCE/CHARACTER/HOPE

Therefore, having been justified by faith, we have peace with God through our Lord Jesus Christ, [2] through whom also we have access by faith into this grace in which we stand, and rejoice in hope of the glory of God. [3] And not only that, but we also glory in tribulations, knowing that tribulation produces perseverance; [4] and perseverance, character; and character, hope. [5] Now hope does not disappoint, because the love of God has been poured out in our hearts by the Holy Spirit who was given to us. Romans 5:1-5 NKJV

The time we are facing is filled with changes and transitions. For some of us it seems like the Lord has exited the room, but even as we know He never leaves us nor forsakes us, we may ask: "What is happening?" Lord you don't show up the way I am used to, and the worship, prayers and intercession seem so different.

These times of transition, are likened unto the moments right before a baby is born, it enters the part of the birth canal where much pressure is experienced.

We are in a time of learning how to preserve and endure, which is extremely important in order to have our characters formed. Every time tribulation and trials come, it is designed to form a stronger character and develop a greater awareness of the hope within us. This is precisely our opportunity to realizing that Jesus Christ in us is the ONLY hope of glory.

Let's look at the caterpillar. It remains in the cocoon until its appointed time, and there is a tremendous struggle to break open and to emerge out of the confinement. This kind of intense struggle develops strength in the butterfly. It will fly freely after coming forth out of this transitional period.

You may feel restrictions and struggles in your life, but we know that Jesus has prepared a place and He has developed something so amazing, that our mouth will be hanging open when we finally see and experience it. That is why Jesus is asking us to come to His table prepared for us, where we are being strengthened and matured to soar with Jesus, knowing all is available to us.

We are coming out of our cocoon as a beautiful butterfly, transformed and reflecting Jesus. It is His glory, His beauty and His essence what we are displaying.

The tension in the Spirit we have felt, is like when Apostle Paul spoke about the pressures within and the pressures without (See 2 Corinthians 11:22-29). There is a storm all around, but we can be in the eye of the storm…resting in Jesus.

In this hour, I sense a refreshing, something new and crisp the Lord is doing. Even the tension has been lifted and something is about to break loose in the Spirit – it is something amazing and we are going from glory to glory and from faith to faith. We see Jesus with unveiled faces and we see the glory of God in the face of Jesus. We are transformed and become more glorious as outlined in 2 Corinthians 3:17-18. Where the Spirit of the Lord is there is freedom, let's rejoice in it this day.

It is a sense as off we are bringing the promises of God to birth, especially some of our prophetic words, we need to focus on. Those prophetic words the Lord is highlighting, are some of the prophecies, we have been given in the past. We need to pick them up and pray them back to Him. There is a need just to lay hold of the promises; He has given us, because there is a bursting forth and a birthing happening presently. Even when a baby is getting ready to be born and is in the birth canal, it is like pushing through a tight tunnel. A transitioning is taking place, which is unfamiliar and uncomfortable.

"Shall I bring to the point of birth, and not give delivery?" says the LORD. "Or shall I who gives delivery shut the womb?" says your God. Isaiah 66:9 NAS

It is time to bring to full fruition and to birth the promises of God in prayer, so that they are manifested in our lives and we can walk in it. It is the season to lay hold of the prophecies; touching and agreeing, as the water breaks right before the baby is born.

The kingdom of God is showcased and His glory is manifested amongst us, and I want to rejoice in that. Don't ever forget the inheritance we have in Christ Jesus and remember the words that were spoken over you, remember the impartations, you have received, remember those who have laid hands on you. I pray that the gifts are stirred up within you and they are fanned to flames!

Every time we encounter adversity we will glory in it, knowing that endurance is formed in us, and this endurance creates a good character and eventually hope is developed and this kind of hope does not disappoint, because the love of God is evident in all of our endeavors trenched in heart-felt love from the Father. This love has been given by the Father and it cannot be taken from us. We will emerge from those times of struggles filled with perseverance and a noble character infused with hope, always reminding us that it is Jesus Christ in us, Who is the hope of glory!

There are many changes and transformations happening in churches and ministries. We have not been this way before and we are being prepared to function according to God's kingdom, because our prayer still is: "Your kingdom come Your will be done on earth as it is in heaven."

Religion and traditions have kept many from the truth about the Gospel of the Kingdom of God, which is to be preached all over the world and then the end of the age will come.

Kingdom mindsets and ways are being put in place and as we are willing to shift with the Lord's agenda, He will place us in a pleasant space, even in a spacious place, where our gifts make room for us. As we already have discussed before, the Body of Christ is being fitly joined together and room is being made for *everyone* to function in their God-given place.

We have been justified by faith and have peace with God through our Lord Jesus Christ. Through Him we also have access by faith into this grace in which we stand, and rejoice in hope of the glory of God (see Romans 5:1-2)

GOLDEN NUGGETS

19

AN EXPECTED OUTCOME

For I know the thoughts that I think toward you, saith the LORD, thoughts of peace, and not of evil, to give you an expected end. Jeremiah 29:11 KJV

In Jeremiah 29:11, God promises "a future and a hope." From the original language that word "future" could be translated "an expected end" or "a ground of hope." In other words, there will be an outcome and there will be completion in your life. God will tie up the loose ends and forming a divine tapestry of your life.

What is the expected outcome?

Well, I woke up with that phrase: An expected outcome. Actually, I woke up at 5:55 am. The number 5 resembles grace and this was a triple number for grace. I love experiencing and receiving God's grace for every day. But what is my expected outcome? At 5:55 am I started praying in the Spirit as I was lying on my bed and it was a little after 7:00 am, the next time I looked at the clock. Where did the time go? I know I did not fall back asleep or did I?

Anyhow, I started praying about this "expected outcome". What came to my mind was that I needed to pray for an expected outcome. I was to pray for the time to be redeemed for the days are evil and for me to walk circumspectly, knowing the will and purposes of God and I was also praying for wisdom about how I was to spend the time given to me each day.

PRIORITIZING YOUR TIME

This is why I am sharing how important it is to prioritize our time and that each one of us has been given 24 hours a day. During those 24 hours, it is up to us on how we use this time effectively for His glory. We are well able and blessed to produce everlasting fruit for the Glory of God.

We have the freedom to choose what we do with our allotted time. Just as Apostle Paul said: "Everything is permissible, but not everything is edifying or beneficial." (See 1 Corinthians 10:23) Therefore, my heart is to seek not my own good, but the good of others. In all of this, I keep His kingdom first and seek to effectively use my time not just to be busy, but to be fruitful! The key to effective use of my time is to move into God's glory and by God-ordained priorities. Keeping the main thing the main thing! One way of doing this is to know how everything is easy in His glory. By moving into the ease of the glory, we can impart what we have obtained and will see others experiencing signs, wonders and miracles.

GOLDEN GLORY BRINGING A HARVEST

The scripture in Jeremiah 29:11 speaks of the good plan and future, God has for us and an expected end, which means that there will be a good outcome. We live in a time where great mysteries are being revealed that will cause an outpouring of God's glory and harvest. His golden glory will bring in a golden harvest! God is searching for those, who will make time to look for the unfolding of a wave of greater glory coupled with a move of holiness. After all, we are blessed with this treasure in earthen vessel and it includes "the knowledge of the glory of the Lord, as the waters cover the sea" (Hab. 2:14). This flood of knowledge is unlocking golden nuggets of hidden realms of glory. Furthermore, He is speaking to us in the following scripture:

I will stand upon my watch, and set me upon the tower, and will watch to see what he will say unto me, and what I shall answer when I am reproved. And the LORD answered me, and said, Write the vision, and make it plain upon tables, that he may run that readeth it. Habakkuk 2:1-2 KJV

Let's be like the prophet Habakkuk. He was a Seer Prophet and he positioned himself to "see" what the Lord was "telling" him and he followed His direction to write down the vision and to make it plain, which means he wrote it down in a manner, that everyone who was reading it, knew instantly if it was a vision to be followed or not. We only desire to have those follow the God-given vision, if it speaks to them and resonates with what they already have been receiving from the Lord.

Let's consider that God's timetable is different than ours. He dwells outside of time and He sees the beginning and the end all at once.

Are you in synch with the Holy Spirit and are you on His timetable?

Can you see the heavens opening and the mysteries of the glory unveiling?

GOLDEN NUGGETS

20

SOARING ON GOD'S GLORY

"But those who hope in the Lord will renew their strength. They will soar on wings like eagles; they will run and not grow weary, they will walk and not be faint. Isaiah 40:31 NIV

Are you ready to soar on wings as eagles and on God's glory? Are you ready to be liberated to soar on higher heights and explore deeper depth with your Beloved, Jesus Christ? It is very important to be able to rise above all the pressures of this world and as Jesus said: "I have overcome this world," so can we overcome the world system, in Him and through Him.

How many times have well-meaning Christians started to drift from the purpose of God and finding themselves frustrated and miserable?

Hosea 4:6 says that God's people perish for lack of vision (knowledge). My vision has to be in Him and my knowledge about His will and glory is in need to be increased, as already mentioned tin this book. According to Habakkuk 2:2, I am to write down the vision, make it plain, keep it before me and then will I be able to remain focused. Along with such focus comes the motivation to continue to seek Jesus and God's kingdom and His righteousness.

Eagles fly so high that they see things from a much different perspective and they possess a unique set of eyes. All birds of prey have excellent long-distance vision, but eagles stand out. They can see clearly and this is part of the prophetic gifting available to us and as we continuously look into Jesus' marvelous eyes; full of life, full of destiny, and full of captivating love, means that we will forever be changed and transformed from glory to glory! It is out of these amazing times of saturation, exaltation and fascination, beholding the glory of Jesus, that we are empowered to run the race with endurance!

Allow yourself to go higher and deeper into His glory and wait for the wind of the Holy Spirit to take you into the heavenly realm. When you enter the Throne room of God through the open door, by the blood of the Lamb, as described in Revelation 4:1, you will be fascinated and start to see and perceive as God does. In His presence the eyes of our heart and understanding are opened and we can see the full, deep and clear knowledge of His will in all spiritual wisdom, in comprehensive insight into the ways and purpose of God and in discernment of spiritual things; so that you may walk, live and conduct yourselves in a manner worthy of the Lord, fully pleasing Him in all things, bearing fruit in every good work and steadily growing and increasing in and by the knowledge of God, with fuller, deeper, and clearer insight, acquaintance, and recognition of His Glory.

Praying that you may be invigorated and strengthened with all power according to the might of His glory, to exercise every kind of endurance and patience perseverance and forbearance with joy." (See Colossians 1:9b-11)

- Filled with knowledge of His will and in all wisdom and spiritual understanding
- Walk worthy of the Lord, fully pleasing Him, being fruitful in every good work
- Increase in the knowledge of God
- Strengthened with all might, according to His glorious power, for all patience and longsuffering with joy

SETTING YOUR MIND ON THE HEAVENLY GLORY REALM

Therefore if you have been raised with Christ [to a new life, sharing in His resurrection from the dead], keep seeking the things that are above, where Christ is, seated at the right hand of God. 2 Set your mind and keep focused habitually on the things above [the heavenly things], not on things that are on the earth [which have only temporal value]. Colossians 3:1-2 AMP

By setting our mind on things above, on the heavenly glory realm and not on the things of earth, which are only temporal and as we keep thinking on things with a good report, God will keep us in His perfect peace.

⤚ **Spread your wings and soar on God's Glory**

GOLDEN NUGGETS

21

PULL OUT ALL THE STOPS

The definition for "pull out all the stops" in the Cambridge English Dictionary is to do everything you can to make something successful. Concerning this nugget, I am talking about releasing the fullness of our destiny planned even before the foundation of the earth - planned way ahead, not by man, but by Almighty God.

The Father planned our destiny not to just randomly fit, but He precisely tailored everything to flow and merge with other streams. These streams can be other people or ministries or callings or business opportunities and places to call your home.

God's appointed time for certain streams to merge is at hand and as we bow to His will in obedience, just as Jesus did while on earth (See Hebrews 5:8), so will we collide with God's perfect plan and purpose in our lives and existence here on earth. Always being aware that we are already living in eternity, knowing we are in this world, but not of it, because our citizenship is in heaven.

Why would we desire for this to happen? It is so that heaven can come and that God's will can be done on earth as it is in heaven. So that we can enjoy Kingdom manifestations and Kingdom revelation in our sphere of influence.

Do you believe it? Can you perceive and receive it?

Divine adjustments are being made, as preparations for this new season in the Lord are underway. Heaven is not sleeping nor slumbering and we are of the day, since Jesus has taken us out of darkness into His marvelous light. He has removed all blindfolds so we can see as He sees, we can taste as He tastes of the heavenly things.

"We are all sons of light and sons of the day. 6 Therefore let us not sleep as others do, but let us watch and be sober." 1 Thessalonians 5:5-6 NKJV

In 1 Thessalonians 5, we are told that the day of the Lord will not overtake us as a thief, because we are sons of the day and sons of the light. This means we have been taken out of satan's domain, the place we used to be, and planted into the kingdom of our Beloved Savior Jesus Christ. He has delivered us and we have a light, because Jesus is the Light of the world. We are partakers of heavenly things and we are asked to be sober, to be watchful and self-controlled, because we are sons (and daughters) of the day.

But if we walk in the light, as he is in the light, we have fellowship with one another, and the blood of Jesus, his Son, purifies us from all sin. 1 John 1:7 NIV

God has not appointed us to wrath, but to obtain salvation through our Lord Jesus Christ. 1 Thessalonians 5:9 NKJV

Everything around us on this earth seems to be changing rapidly, and the Bride of Christ is making herself ready to be without spot or wrinkles. The Lord is bringing the different streams, representing the various callings, together and we are merging with the ones prepared to be fitly joined.

Being of the day means to walk with Jesus, to abide in Him and to receive what He reveals to us and to swim in His divine River of Life to accomplish on earth what has been planned and already exists in heaven.

"Pulling out all the stops" reminds me of the radical moves we have seen in the past church history. For example, the reformation in Martin Luther's time. This monk caused a radical shift and a transforming change for multitudes and it has impacted every continent.

Are we prepared to flow with the requirements of the kingdom of God? Am I willing to be obedient to my heavenly call? Even Jesus, when on earth, learned obedience through the things He suffered. (See Hebrews 5:8).

Suffering is actually a freeing word. Suffering for the sake of the Gospel of the Kingdom of God and for Jesus Christ is an extremely fruitful and honorable thing. Laying down ones live freely, even during much persecution, is the ultimate sacrifice. Jesus did exactly such and He is asking us to pick up our cross daily and follow Him. But the idea about denying ourselves does not mix with some of the teachings we have received in this age.

Then Jesus said to those Jews who believed Him, "If you abide in My word, you are my disciples indeed. And you shall know the truth and the truth shall make you free." John 8:31-32 NKJV

We can rejoice that we have been delivered from the desire to be sons of the night and the deeds of darkness. We are not to misunderstand that, being sons of the day, does not mean we never sleep physically. However, our spirit man is alert in Him on a consistent basis. Communication with my Lord is never interrupted and actually I am to make Him my dwelling place. He is my home and I am His home. He is in me and I am in Him and greater is He, who is within us, than he who is in the world!

It is such a joy to be the ambassador of Christ and to be a co-laborer with Him. Forever intertwined with Him and tasting the good word of God and the powers of the age to come. (See Hebrews 6:5)

In a practical sense, we live each day unto Him and no matter what is coming our way, we know that we can do all things through Christ, Who strengthens us. This strength does not come from our own efforts, instead it comes by using faith to rise into the glory realm and to do what we see God doing and hence there will be immediate and lasting results.

22

SPEAKING BOLDLY MAKING KNOWN THE MYSTERY OF THE GOSPEL

Paul asked in *Ephesians 6:19: "Pray for me, that utterance may be given to me, that I may open my mouth boldly to make known the mystery of the gospel..."*

"Continue earnestly in prayer, being vigilant in it with thanksgiving; meanwhile praying also for us, that God would open to us a door for the word, to speak the mystery of Christ, for which I am also in chains." Colossians 4:2-3 NKJV

It was very important to Paul that he was effective in communicating the hidden truth of the gospel of the kingdom of God. Effective Communication depends not just on the words we speak, but also in demonstration of the Spirit and power.

Paul always emphasized, that he did not come with eloquence of speech or with persuasive word of human wisdom, but with the demonstration of the power of God, so that the faith should not be in the wisdom of men but in the power of God. (See 1 Corinthians 2:4)

In Romans 1:16 he said that he is not ashamed of the gospel of Christ, for it is the power of God to salvation for everyone who believes, for the Jews first and also for the Greek.

Paul had a divine desire and knew he was to visit Rome and he expressed it:

"For I long to see you, that I may impart to you some spiritual gift, so that you may be established - that is, that I may be encouraged together with you by the mutual faith both of you and me." Romans 1:11-12 NKJV

Years ago in one of the Soaring Eagle newsletters, I outlined an upcoming conference, which was taking place in Paris, where I was scheduled to be a speaker. It is extremely difficult to explain how elated I was about this open door of opportunity. For years I prayed about returning to France and I was longing to connect with the brethren in France, so I could impart some spiritual gifts and to minister in the Word of God, as well as seeing the demonstration of the Spirit and power.

As I was interceding, declaring and prophesying over Paris and France, the Holy Spirit proclaimed that ancient strongholds of the enemy are broken and the light of Jesus Christ is coming to penetrate the darkness. Years prior to this, I flew over France on my way to Frankfurt, Germany. I saw dense fog clouding France and realized that the god of this world had darkened and blinded the people to prevent them from believing.

"Whose minds the god of this age has blinded, who do not believe, lest the light of the Gospel of the glory of Christ, who is the image of God, should shine on them."
2 Corinthians 4:4 NKJV

In the Spirit, I also saw an opening over Paris! The radiance of the sun (Son) was above the clouds, but the people on the earth could not see the splendor, because of the fog and this signifies that spiritually their minds are blinded.

So how do we pray for those people? We pray that the blindness will be taken away, so that the light of the gospel of the glory of Christ, who is the image of God, should shine on them. As the Spirit of the Lord is stirring within you, please pray for your family, your neighborhood and your nation and everything else the Lord is placing on your heart.

➢ Pray that utterance may be given to boldly make known the mystery of the gospel.
➢ Pray that God would open a door for the word, to speak the mystery of Christ.
➢ Signs and wonders to follow the preaching of the word
➢ Pray for the blindness of their minds to be removed so that the light of the gospel of the glory of Christ, who is the image of God, should shine

GOLDEN NUGGETS

23

RENEW YOUR SPIRITUAL VITALITY

"Therefore strengthen the hands which hang down, and the feeble knees, and make straight paths for your feet, so that what is lame may not be dislocated, but rather be healed." Hebrews 12:12-13 NKJV

Years ago, I was placed in a leadership position for a large international ministry. The position required to oversee various lighthouses across several counties in the state of Florida. Each lighthouse had its own set of local leaders. The above scripture was given to me by the Lord and as I pondered what He was trying to say, I realized that many of the local leaders' encountered setbacks and that their hands were hanging down. The hands hanging down represented discouragement and hope deferred and it can make the heart sick. Additionally, the knees of some were feeble and without any spiritual vitality and strength. What was lacking was that which is to be supplied within the body of Christ (see Ephesians 4).

Immediately I sensed to invite all the leaders and "Fresh Fire meetings" were held. These meetings were designed to bring them all together and a strengthening took place as they were ministered to and as a sense of belonging returned. New friendships among them formed and old friendships rekindled. Soon the spiritual vitality returned to these living organisms within this part of the body of Christ!

Where do you belong in the body of Christ? It seems to be high time for each one to find and locate our places in the fellowship of the saints.

Who is the Lord joining you to? As a body part we need to find our place as we allow the Lord to join us and receive life giving, spiritual connectivity!

Connections, connections, connections.

Make straight paths. Walk circumspectly, walk humbly and remain on the narrow path, Jesus charted out for us. So that what is lame, those places not functioning, lifeless and without having the required strength, will not be dislocated, but rather be healed.

Picture the agony of a dislocated shoulder! This shoulder is out of joint and will not be healed until it is returned to where it belongs.

"Pursue peace with all people, and holiness without which no one will see the Lord: looking carefully lest anyone fall short of the grace of God; lest any root of bitterness springing up cause trouble, and by this many become defiled." Hebrews 12:14-15 NKJV

Let's pursue peace and holiness as we look out for one another in love and with the grace of the Lord. We cannot afford to allow negative emotions like resentment, self-pity, and un-forgiveness to build up within us. These emotions will turn into a root of bitterness and actually poison everyone around us. Holiness unto the Lord requires a sanctification process, as we allow the Refiner's fire to burn off the dross and the Fuller's soap to cleanse us. The blood of Jesus still contains the power to cleanse us from all sin, as we confess. He is faithful and just to forgive our sins and cleanse us from all unrighteousness (See 1 John 1:9).

Most likely everyone has felt the sting of a root of bitterness, as we have become the recipient of someone's wrath, anger and bitterness. We can only overcome this kind of attack by loving others. Therefore, we endeavor to love God with all our heart, mind, soul and strength and love our neighbor as we love ourselves.

Furthermore, be earnest, unwearied and steadfast in your prayer life, being both alert and intent in your forgiving and praying coupled with thanksgiving. (See Colossians 4:2) This kind of fervency will keep you moving in the love of God and will remove all bitterness.

☛ Allow the Holy Spirit to renew your spiritual vitality!

GOLDEN NUGGETS

24

ARMOR OF RIGHTEOUSNESS

While spending time with the Lord this morning, I came across the scripture in 2 Corinthians 6, where Apostle Paul spoke about the "marks of ministry". He was pleading with those who work together with the Lord, not to receive the grace of God for nothing.

As I was reading about all the various warnings Apostle Paul drew attention to; topics like not being offended, being blameless, exercising much patience and endurance, in tribulations, needs and in distress, as well as imprisonments, in tumults, and in sleeplessness, to name just a few, I sensed I needed to pay special attention to the "power in the word of truth, the power of God and the armor of righteousness on the right hand and on the left." (See 2 Corinthians 6:7)

When I ponder on the armor of righteousness, I immediately thought of the scripture in Ephesians 6 teaching about the full armor of God. It all points to the armor the Roman soldiers wore in those days. The spear or sword was carried in the right hand as an offensive weapon. The shield, on the other hand, was a defensive weapon. It was designed to provide protection against the enemy.

These Roman soldiers went well armed and trained to the battle. So do we, as the saints of God, we are to be well trained and equipped to meet conflicts like encountering persecution, slander and opposition! We do not fight against flesh and blood as the Roman soldiers did, but we are well armed spiritually by wielding skillfully the Word of God and holding up the shield of faith in order to quench the fiery darts of the enemy.

In actual fact, the Lord said in Zechariah 2:5 ESV: "And I will be to her a wall of fire all around, declares the LORD, and I will be the glory in her midst.' We also know that His Glory is our rear-guard and will protect us from behind.

Furthermore, I like to point out once again that we withstand and overcome trials and conflict by behaving in all things as the ministers of God. For example to accomplish this, it requires the wearing of the armor of righteousness on the right and left hand. Especially as leaders in ministry, the armor with which we face the enemy is marked first and foremost by a holy and pure life. It is our defense by living a life marked by purity, by knowledge, by longsuffering, by kindness, by the Holy Spirit, by sincere love, by the word of truth, by the power of God, and by the armor of righteousness on the right hand and on the left. (See 2 Corinthians 6:6-7)

We have no swords, spears, helmets, nor shields, no carnal weapons of offense and defense, nevertheless we expect to conquer all of the assaults, and to gain all victories, by the blood of Jesus Christ, the word of truth, the power of God and an upright and holy life according to Apostle Paul's teaching.

As believers in the finished work of the cross and as followers of Jesus Christ, we are already the righteousness of God in Christ Jesus and we are exhorted to continue our walk by faith in Christ and to be holy as He is holy. (See 2 Corinthians 5:21)

Pure and holy lives are our defensive weapon of righteousness on our left hand!

Wielding the word of truth and demonstrating the power of God is our offensive weapon of righteousness on the right hand!

GOLDEN NUGGETS

25

JESUS CHRIST WAS CRUCIFIED, BURIED, RESURRECTED AND ASCENDED

Every year especially during the Resurrection weekend, I am reminded again about the time I had a vision being in the tomb, where Jesus' dead body was laying.

At first it was dark, and then suddenly the glory of God, as beams of brilliant light, like lasers, entered the tomb consuming the darkness. The resurrection power of the Holy Spirit appeared along with many angels and Jesus' body was resurrected from the dead.

I saw Jesus removing the face cloth, which was placed on His face and around His head, and He ever so gently and lovingly folded it and placed it not with His burial cloth, but in a place by itself.

Let me explain what I found out about the face cloth lying beside the burial clothes in the tomb. Honestly, up to the time of this encounter, I have read the four Gospels numerous times, but never caught the description of this incidence. In the book of John I finally found the answer!

The Gospel of John (20:7) tells us that the cloth, which was placed over the face of Jesus, was not just thrown aside like the grave clothes. The Bible takes an entire verse to tell us that the napkin was wrapped together, and was in a place by itself.

"So they ran both together: and the other disciple did outrun Peter, and came first to the sepulchre. And he stooping down, and looking in, saw the linen clothes lying; yet went he not in. Then cometh Simon Peter following him, and went into the sepulchre, and seeth the linen clothes lie, And the napkin, that was about his head, not lying with the linen clothes, but wrapped together in a place by itself. Then went in also that other disciple, which came first to the sepulchre, and he saw, and believed." John 20:4-8 KJV

WHY IS THIS SO VERY IMPORTANT?

When I had this vision and afterwards prayed for additional understanding, I realized, that just as the curtain separating the Holy of Holies in the Temple was rent in two from the top to the bottom during the death of Jesus Christ on the cross, so was the face cloth removed from the face of Jesus, giving entrance to have face to face encounters with Him.

As we know, this curtain was too strong for anyone to tear it in two, especially from the top to the bottom.

Therefore, it is a known fact that it was done supernaturally to open the way through Jesus Christ and His precious blood into the Holy of Holies. Therefore, we can now come boldly to the Throne of Grace. Jesus is the Way, the Truth and Life and made a way for us to come to the Father and to enter His presence. (See John 14:6)

"After this I looked, and behold, a door standing open in heaven! And the first voice, which I had heard speaking to me like a trumpet, said, "Come up here, and I will show you what must take place after this." *Revelation 4:1 ESV*

WITH UNVEILED FACES BEHOLDING THE GLORY OF THE LORD

In 2 Corinthians 3, we can read about the veil placed upon the minds or hearts of those who are under the law. Nevertheless, when one turns to the Lord, the veil is lifted or taken away.

I witnessed His resurrection and will never forget the impact this had on my walk with Him. The intentional removal and folding of the face cloth signifies the face to face encounters we can have with Jesus through His sacrifice and through those intimate times with Him, a mighty transformation occurs within us and we are changed from glory to glory.

It is breath-taking and warms my heart to be able to see into His eyes and to smell His fragrance, as I am so very close to Him. Not only can I enjoy Jesus, but He also made the way for me to come to the Father. I can see the knowledge of the glory of God in the face of Jesus Christ!

"We all, with unveiled face, beholding as in a mirror the glory of the Lord, are being transformed into the same image from glory to glory, just as by the Spirit of the Lord. 2 Corinthians 3:18 NKJV

For God, who said, "Let light shine out of darkness," has shone in our hearts to give the light of the knowledge of the glory of God in the face of Jesus Christ." 2 Corinthians 4:6 ESV

ASCENDED LIFE

It is absolutely vital to realize that Jesus was not only crucified, buried and resurrected but He also ascended into heaven. Jesus Christ was not dead; it was only His physical body that died. Could it be true, that while His body lay in the tomb, He retrieved the keys of death and Hades?

"I am the Living One; I was dead, and behold I am alive for ever and ever! And I hold the keys of death and Hades." Revelation 1:18 NIV

Jesus ascended into heaven and we, who are hidden in Him, are privileged to live an ascended lifestyle. Until Jesus comes back, the same way the disciples saw Him go into heaven, we are not bound to earth as some may think. We can live and walk in His Spirit and have been given His authority and life. All of this combined, including the finished work of the Cross, gives us permission to be living from heavenly places and not towards heaven. Actually, we are partnering with the Holy Spirit, so that we have a consciousness or awareness of the presence of God that takes us into a place of majesty were we abide. An elevated presence of God within empowers us and we are citizens of heaven and are not succumbing to the ways of the world system around us. We access the favor of God and we can release Heaven on earth, as we live in a consistent way in the power of the Holy Spirit.

"BECAUSE I LIVE, YOU ALSO WILL LIVE."

~ JESUS

Now when He had spoken these things, while they watched, He was taken up, and a cloud received Him out of their sight. [10] And while they looked steadfastly toward heaven as He went up, behold, two men stood by them in white apparel, [11] who also said, "Men of Galilee, why do you stand gazing up into heaven? This same Jesus, who was taken up from you into heaven, will so come in like manner as you saw Him go into heaven." ACTS 1:9-12 NKJV

GOLDEN NUGGETS

26

DOMINION AT THE GATE

"Thus says the Lord to His anointed, to Cyrus, whose right hand I have held to subdue nations before him, and I will unarm and ungird the loins of kings to open doors before him, so that gates will not be shut. 2 I will go before you and level the mountains (to make the crooked places straight); I will break in pieces the doors of bronze and cut asunder the bars of iron. 3 And I will give you the treasures of darkness, and hidden riches of secret places, that you may know that it is I, the Lord, the God of Israel, Who calls you by your name." Isaiah 45:1 AMPC

There has never been a more exhilarating time in the history of God's kingdom. The Lord has been equipping His people to be well able to take the mountain of challenge and to overcome in Jesus Christ. The Lord has anointed us to go through every gate of opportunity for effectual ministry that opens before us. We are receiving greater grace and more favor for the increase of authority received in Him.

Many saints have been pruned (see John 15), only to produce more excellent fruit for the glory of God. Through this pruning process, nothing has been lost, only those things we do not need and have been clinging to us. After this release, they are free to enter into a new season of acceleration.

Everything has been gained, as we have proclaimed: "Not my will be done, but YOURS..." and "I give my body as a living sacrifice, holy and acceptable unto You." There has been a deep resolve for many to only live for, and to love Him first.

The gate represents a place where the king's authority was implemented, issues of culture, commerce, and military strategies were decided, and judicial renderings were released.

The Bride of Christ stands ready with keys in her hands, anointed to unlock the gates of earth, in order to establish His "Kingdom". Jesus already opened the gates of heaven, but many treasures are yet to be unearthed globally.

"And I tell you, you are Peter, and on this rock I will build My church, and the gates of hell shall not overpower it. 19 I will give you the keys of the kingdom of heaven; and whatever you bind (declare to be improper and unlawful) on earth must be what is already bound in heaven; and whatever you lose (declare lawful) on earth must be what is already loosed in heaven."
Matthew 16:18 AMPC

JESUS CHRIST is building His church; He is doing it, not anyone else. Therefore, the gates of hell shall not prevail against the kingdom of God. There shall be no end to the increase of His government! We have the keys of authority to open every gate set before us and we can receive fresh revelation from the Lord continually. (See Jeremiah 33:3).

We are His gatekeepers in our region and what we deem proper and lawful will be allowed, but everything not allowed in heaven, will be forbidden on earth. As gatekeepers we are stewards and are responsible to release God's Truth through our gate.

"These things says He who is holy, He who is true, "He who has the key of David, He who opens and no one shuts, and shuts and no one opens" Revelation 3:7

It is the time of apostolic reformation. Greater wisdom is revealed for divine strategies on how to advance the Kingdom of God, even releasing His fire to ignite a Global Awakening. Therefore listen to and meditate on what the Spirit of God is saying. (See Revelations 3:8, 10-13)

ANGELIC VISITATIONS

It is imperative to engage with the angelic host and to understand the significance of being in unity and agreement with what the Father is doing on earth.

I am well aware that when I discovered the pebbles and they turned into golden nuggets, angels were present to precipitate it. Just as in Bible days, angelic visitations are profound experiences, which often mark the opening of new gates. Angels deliver messages, as they did in the case of Daniel and they bring not only direction, but also strategies and insight. Those instructions will empower us to receive dominion at the gates and to execute God's authority.

"All authority in heaven and on earth has been given to me, "Jesus said. (Matthew 28:18 NIV)

Exousia, the Greek word for "authority," means "rightful, actual and unimpeded power to act, possess, control or dispose of someone or something."

Jesus used His authority to disarm the enemy and all his demonic forces and powers. "And having disarmed the powers and authorities, he made a public spectacle of them, triumphing over them by the cross." (Col. 2:15)

He stripped the enemy of all his rights and we are well able to partner with the Holy Spirit to establish God's kingdom in the gates!

27

BEWARE OF THE POLITICAL SPIRIT

"Be careful," Jesus warned. "Watch out for the yeast of the Pharisees and that of Herod." Mark 8:15 NIV

It seems that there is an increase in disunity among believers. Could it be that there is a spiritual force at work that many believers are falling for? Paul recognized this with the church at Corinth (1 Corinthians 11:18). As we are facing a lot of discord, disunity, disjointedness, criticism, slander and backbiting among our brothers and sisters world-wide, I have been asking the Lord for wisdom and insight. What are we really dealing with? What is the underlying cause for such carnal fruit?

At first I thought it was solely the spirit of Jezebel, but the Holy Spirit gave me discernment and pointed to the scripture in Mark 8:15. In this exhortation, I will be focusing on the leaven of Herod. Jesus warned us to be careful and to watch out for the yeast of the Pharisees and that of Herod.

What was He talking about? Most of us know and have heard teachings on the religious or Pharisaical spirit, but many are not aware of the Political spirit. Why did

Jesus speak about the Roman king Herod, who had become the ruler of the Jews?

Herod knew of the prophecies of a coming Messiah, who would one day set up His kingdom and liberate the people. This kingdom would have no end. Herod therefore, spoke to the Wise Men and wanted to find out where this King was to be born. He even told them that he desired to go and worship this new King. Yet Herod had another plan and it was to annihilate this rival and when the Wise Men did not come back to him, Herod out of fear and hatred sent out a decree that all children two years and younger must be killed. The political spirit will release threats and decrees that will instill fear and possibly cause believers to abort their Kingdom assignments in their lives and regions.

After the birth of Jesus, Joseph and Mary were warned by an angel and told to travel to Egypt. This was to protect Jesus from Herod's plot.

"Get up, take the young child and his mother and flee to Egypt, and stay there until I give you word, for Herod is about to search for the young child to kill him." *Matthew 2:13*

Remember Herod said to the Three Wise Men, he desired to go and worship the new King! This was a lie and this spirit attacks and tries to kill, steal and destroy in a sly, crafty, cunning way and makes it look like it is a good thing.

DIVISION VS. UNITY

One of the strategies and schemes of the enemy is always to divide and conquer (See 2 Corinthians 2:11). We as believers must be diligent and quick to recognize this tactic and not give in to it. Instead we are asked to maintain the unity of the Spirit in the bond of peace. This is accomplished by forgiving one another and walking in love. (See Ephesians 4:1-5) A unity of the Body of Christ is going to be manifested that can be described as miraculous. Many groups that have been separated in the past, because of doctrinal differences or offenses, are finding themselves unified through the manifested glory.

Many leaders of groups have seen the need for unity, and have tried to work on this problem. Some well-known leaders of ministries testify that the key to an effective ministry is unity.

I have known the leaders of a church in a town in Germany for many years. It has been miraculous to witness how those leaders would get together and remain with one another until all disunity and misunderstanding was cleared amongst them. Sometimes when necessary, they stayed half of the night to confess, repent and if need be to "wash each other's feet." They did not leave each other's presence until everything that represented division in their heart was removed and they focused and allowed the glory of God to restore pure and divine unity.

This congregation is well known in the town and they have had tremendous influence on the governmental aspect of the city and have reconciled many to Christ!

TARGETING THE PROPHETIC

The political spirit will want to associate with the prophetic and with the sons of God. This spirit will declare that the focus is on worshipping and glorifying God, yet the true agenda is to sooth the expectations of the people. This all is fueled by fear and rejection. After King Saul, out of fear of losing his grip, he requested that Prophet Samuel remain with him, so that the people would be appeased. He wanted the people to think he is still in charge. He was portraying a kingdom, but it was not in alignment with God's kingdom and its blueprint. He wanted to associate with someone, who was in right standing with the Lord, in order to conceal his own trespasses. The political spirit will try to align with the prophetic mantle to cover up its own agenda and relentless scheming. It will even appear to be right on target with God's purpose and seems to be accurate, but behind the scene it is filled with wrong agendas and has endeavored to bring disunity and confusion amongst God's children, ultimately targeting to stifle God's kingdom. (See 1 Samuel 15:24-26)

THE SIGNS OF A POLITICAL SPIRIT

The political spirit seeks to captivate minds and operates by mere carnal reasoning and opinions. This spirit separates people into two categories; the superior gene and the inferior gene.

The political spirit tries to demolish anyone, who is not in agreement. This spirit is more concerned with being right and pushing its ungodly agenda than with obeying the will of the Father.

The political spirit seeks to replace complete loyalty to our Lord, and requires utter surrender to follow and bow down to its agenda. This attitude creates a culture, in which we are forbidden to think for ourselves. Instead we are expected to agree fully with this spirit. Decisions are made solely by affiliation.

This spirit is not easily detected and only with eyes wide open through discernment by the Holy Spirit. Don't engage a battle with it in the flesh. It looks for jealousy, selfish ambition and envy in us, therefore search your heart and repent and turn from its influence and lay down your own will. Because it looks for shady motives to move through and protects its territory. It tries to deceive mediocre Christians.

As we speak about a spirit, remember we do not fight against flesh and blood! It's not the people we target, but the spirit in operation. The Lord will unclothe it and reveal the truth to us, as we ask for discernment and seek Him for answers.

Psalm 133 explains where the blessings of God are found in full force, is where brethren dwell in unity! There might be divisions amongst the brethren in your city or region, but do not fall for this scheme. Keep yourself free from disunity and continue to follow Jesus, His wisdom, His call on your live and the fellowship in the Light.

GOLDEN NUGGETS

ABOUT THE AUTHOR

Gabriele Gilpin, an ordained minister and graduate of Rhema Bible School, is the President and Founder of Soaring Eagle Ministries, Inc.

During her 25+ years of ministry, she has also served as an apostolic lighthouse leader and overseer, traveling preacher, teacher, conference speaker, translator, missionary and author.

Her vision is international and a part of building the Kingdom of God. The vision includes equipping, training and releasing the saints, to do the work of ministering toward building up Christ's body according to Ephesians 4:12, and to truly "soar on wings as eagles." Many have been transformed by the demonstration of the power of God and His Word.

She has been passionate about developing leadership internationally and has been on television, radio and is hosting an internet radio show. Gabriele has seen numerous salvations, miracles, healings, deliverances, signs and wonders following the preaching of the Word. God's anointing on this ministry has been instrumental in helping many individuals to stir up and release the God-given gifts within them in order to start walking in God's calling and purposes for their lives. The preaching, teaching and prayer ministry releases the fire of the Holy Spirit and a prophetic voice to the hearer.

Gabriele served in Aglow International for nearly 15 years starting in 1991 and was president of Aglow lighthouses in New Jersey, and Florida. She pioneered and started the Aglow lighthouse in Hillsborough, New Jersey, as well as serving on the Northeast Florida Area Team of Aglow International.

Presently, both she and her husband are living in Florida.

For speaking engagements, Gabriele Gilpin can be contacted by email, phone or the website.

For more information, to partner with us, or to be added to the mailing list, please contact us:

Soaring Eagle Ministries, Inc.
10990 Ft. Caroline Road # 350352,
Jacksonville, FL 32225

Website: www.soaringeagleinc.org
Email: info@soaringeagleinc.org
Follow the Blog: www.soaringeagleinc.org/blog
Like us on the Facebook Page:
https://www.facebook.com/SoaringEagleMinistries

LIFE TRANSFORMING RESOURCES
FROM SOARING EAGLE MINISTRIES

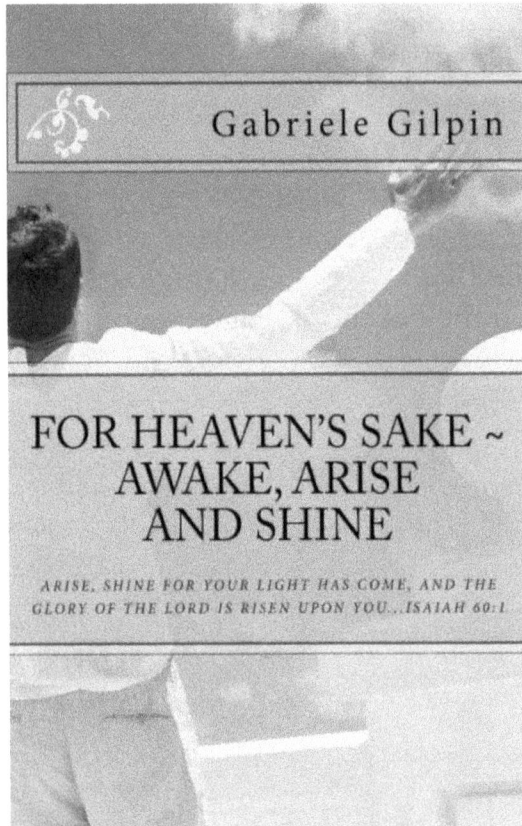

Gabriele Gilpin

FOR HEAVEN'S SAKE ~
AWAKE, ARISE
AND SHINE

ARISE, SHINE FOR YOUR LIGHT HAS COME, AND THE
GLORY OF THE LORD IS RISEN UPON YOU...ISAIAH 60:1

DELIGHT IN THE FATHEROF GLORY

By Gabriele Gilpin

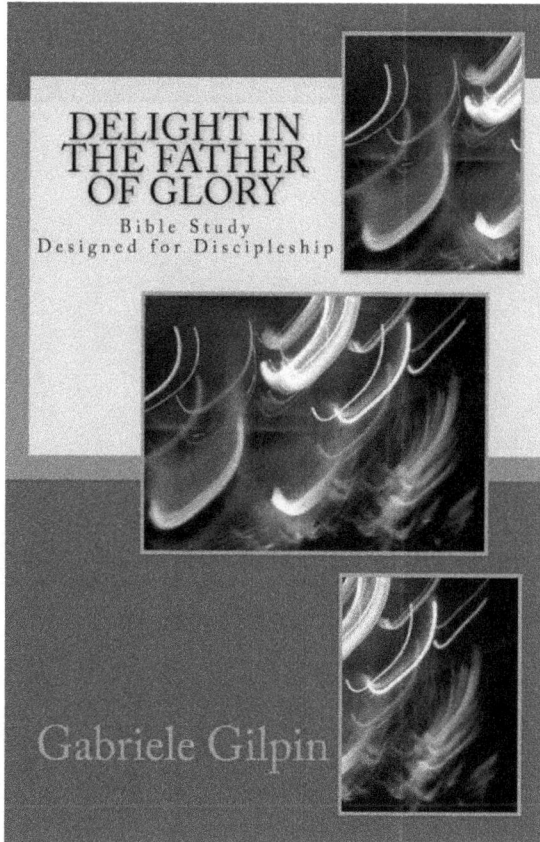

IMPACT THROUGH
FRESH INSIGHT
By Gabriele Gilpin

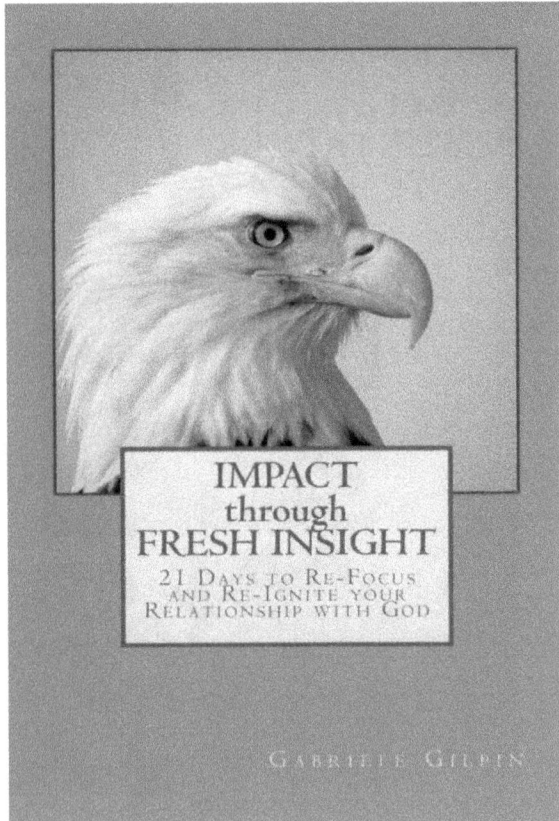

IMPACT
through
FRESH INSIGHT
21 Days to Re-Focus
and Re-Ignite your
Relationship with God

GABRIELE GILPIN

BLAZING FIRE OF THE FATHER'S LOVE
DAILY DEVOTIONAL

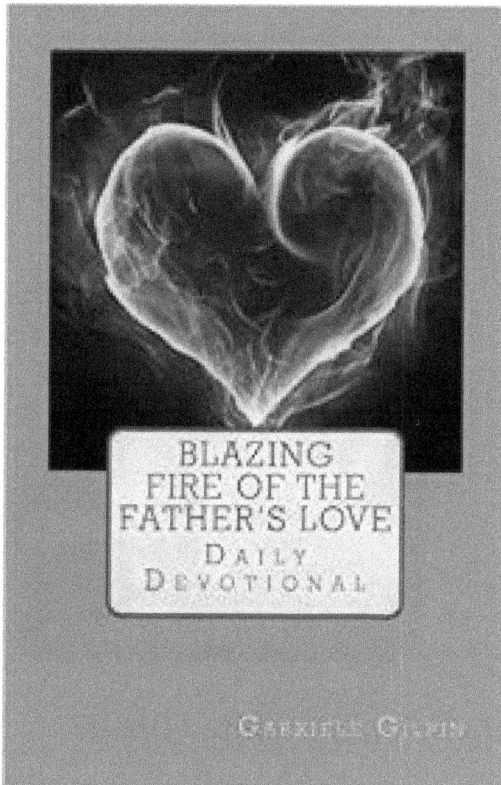

SOARING EAGLE
SCHOOL OF THE SPIRIT I

If interested books can be order on Amazon.com

ALSO IN FRENCH

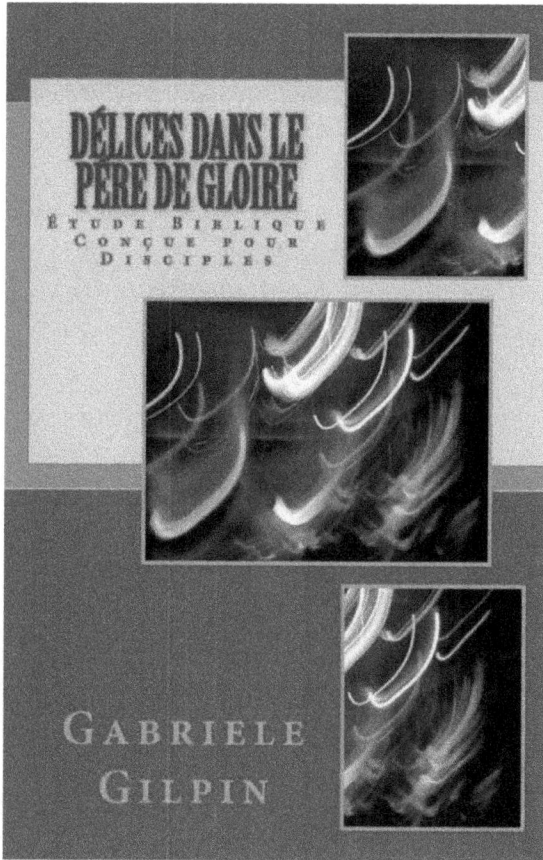

If interested books can be ordered on
Amazon.com

ALSO IN FRENCH

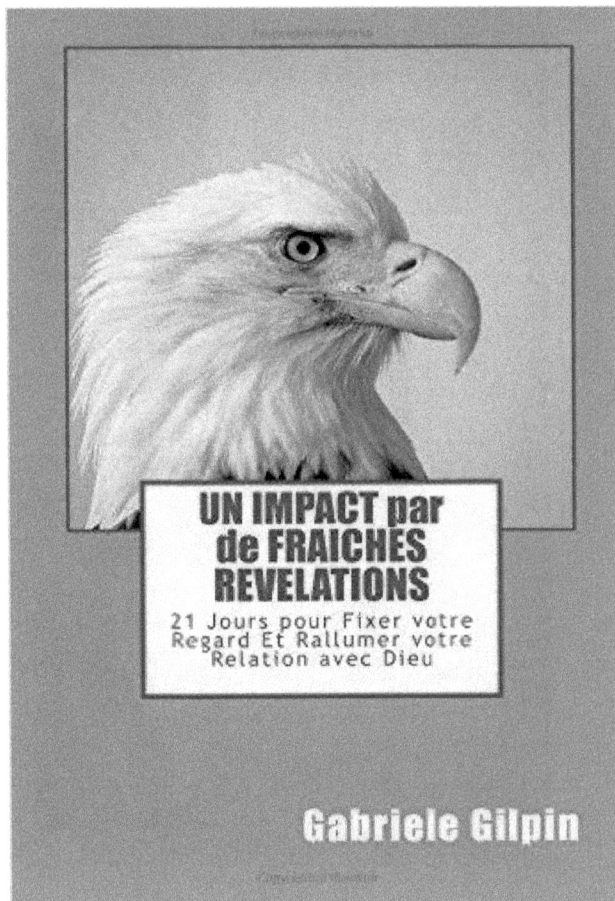

If interested books can be ordered on
Amazon.com